P9-BBQ-578

THE DEAD SEA SCROLLS AND THE BIBLE

THE DEAD SEA SCROLLS AND THE BIBLE

by
Charles F. Pfeiffer

WEATHERVANE BOOKS
NEW YORK

Library of Congress Catalog Card Number: 72-76780

This edition is published by Weathervane Books,
distributed by Crown Publishers, Inc.,
by arrangement with Baker Book House Company
Manufactured in the United States of America
ISBN: 0-517-17491X
u t s r q p o

PREFACE

The reader of this book will want to have beside it a translation of the Scrolls. Millar Burrows' two books, *The Dead Sea Scrolls,* and *More Light on the Dead Sea Scrolls* (Viking Press) were early accessible to English readers, and they provided pioneer translations of the first texts studied by scholars who had access to the Scrolls. In the World *Meridian Books* series is a volume of translation and interpretation by A. Dupont-Sommer, *The Essene Writings from Qumran.* An *Anchor Books* translation, sometimes in the form of paraphrase, entitled *The Dead Sea Scriptures* was written by Theodor H. Gaster. Such works always indicate the views of the translators, but they can be useful tools for study when judiciously used.

It was my privilege to study the Scrolls in two seminars with the late Professor Ralph Marcus of the University of Chicago. Many of the ideas here expressed result from that study. For other suggestions I am indebted to the many scholars who have written concerning the scrolls in such journals as *The Biblical Archaeologist, The Bulletin of the American Schools of Oriental Research, The Jewish Quarterly Review, Revue Biblique, Revue de Qumran, Israel Exploration Journal,* and *Journal of Biblical Literature* The *Revue de Qumran,* published in Paris, contains definite bibliographies edited by Dr. William S. LaSor of Fuller Seminary.

Quotations in this volume indicate the page and line of the

published texts from Qumran, except for the Habbakuk Commentary, where the Biblical chapter and verse divisions are indicated. In the arrangement of subject matter some repetition seemed inevitable. Certain topics are treated in the textual discussions, prior to fuller topical treatment.

The author acknowledges with gratitude the editorial assistance of Mr. Gordon De Young and Mr. Cornelius Zlystra. Acknowledgment of the sources of illustrations is given with each photograph. The helpfulness of friends and organizations which made available the illustrations is deeply appreciated.

Charles F. Pfeiffer

CONTENTS

Illustrations

THE DEAD SEA SCROLLS
AND
THE BIBLE

1

DISCOVERIES IN THE JUDEAN CAVES

In the spring of 1947, in the Judean wilderness, near the northwestern corner of the Dead Sea ancient manuscripts were found which have helped us to reconstruct the history of pre-Christian Judaism. They have also given us our oldest manuscripts of most of the Old Testament.

When these important finds first came to the attention of the world of scholarship, varying theories of their origin and date were advanced, and a "battle of the scrolls" ensued. In seeking to place the scrolls in their proper historical context, scholars remembered reports of other "cave finds" and asked themselves whether the thousands of fragments subsequently pieced together and studied by scholars in the Palestine Museum, Jerusalem, were related to a library which had been raided at least twice before.

I. Origen

Less than three centuries after Christ, the church father Origen (A.D. 185-254) mentioned the discovery of Greek and Hebrew manuscripts found stored in jars in the region of Jericho. Origen's great contribution to Biblical studies was a work known as the Hexapla, an arrangement in parallel columns of the Hebrew and Greek versions extant in his day. The first column of the Hexapla contained the Hebrew text of the Old Testament. The next column gave a transliteration of the Hebrew into Greek. Next followed the Greek translations of Aquila, Symmachus, the Septuagint, and Theodotion. For the Book of Psalms, Origen added three other Greek translations including one found near Jericho. According to Origen's own statement, quoted by

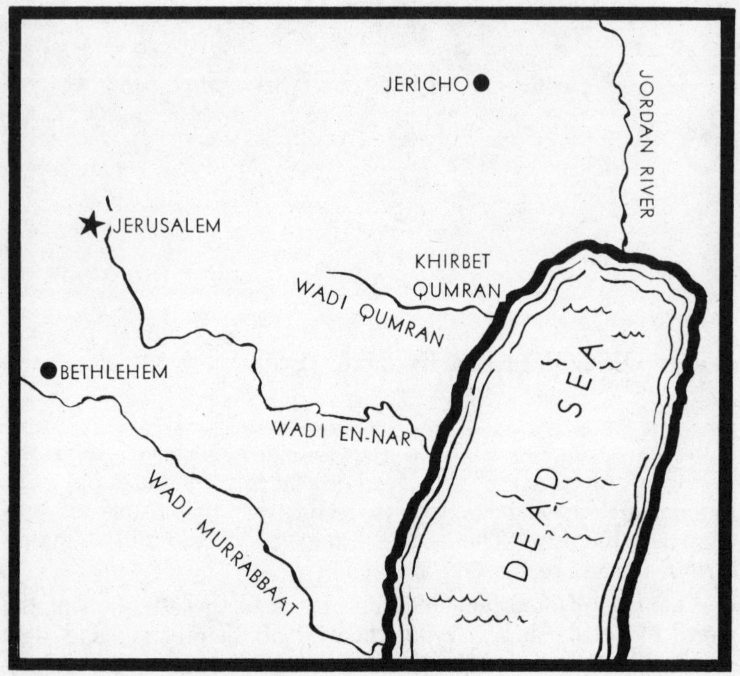

MAP OF THE NORTHERN SECTOR of the Dead Sea showing Khirbet Qumran and its environs.

Eusebius the church historian, he used "the sixth edition which was found together with other Hebrew and Greek books in a jar near Jericho in the reign of Antonius the son of Severus" (A.D. 198-217).

II. Timotheus

About eight hundred years after Christ, the Nestorian Patriarch Timotheus I wrote a letter to Sergius, the Metropolitan of Elam, in which he described the discovery of a large number of Hebrew manuscripts in a cave near Jericho. The story of this earlier "discovery" is strikingly similar to stories of recent finds. Timotheus writes that a Bedouin's dog went into a cave after a sheep. When the dog failed to return the Bedouin entered the cave and found a large library of Biblical and non-Biblical books. The Jews of Jerusalem showed considerable interest in these finds. Scholars suggested that this discovery had important bearings on the theology of the Karaites, the medieval Jewish sect which rejected the rabbinical interpretation of Scripture.

The Jewish Karaite writer, Kirkisani, in a history of the Jewish sects written about the year 937, speaks of a sect known as *al-Maghariya,* "the cave people." He states that the name was given to this sect because its books were found in a cave. The sect was already extinct when Kirkisani wrote. According to the Moslem writer Shahrastani, the "cave people" flourished around the middle of the first century before Christ.

III. Cave 1, Qumran

The modern discovery of manuscripts in caves, presumably in the same area as those of earlier times, begins in the spring of 1947. The stories of the discovery differ in detail, and it may never be possible to tell exactly what happened. Most of the stories tell of an Arab lad, Muhammed-ad-Dhib ("Mohammed the wolf") who was herding goats or sheep in the area. According to one version, a runaway goat entered a cave, whereupon Muhammed threw a stone into the cave. The stone broke a jar, frightening the lad away from the cave. However, Muhammed soon returned with a companion, entered the cave, and found the documents which were to cause such a stir in the world of scholarship. Other stories suggest that Muhammed and a companion took refuge in the cave from a thunderstorm, perhaps while smuggling goods from across the Jordan to Bethlehem. It is easy to understand why other accounts of their activities were given, if they were engaged in illicit business. Later reports suggest that the scrolls may have been found as early as 1945.

The scrolls were brought to Bethlehem, the nearest market town, and attempts were made to sell them. After initial disappointments, a Syrian merchant, thinking the scrolls might be written in Syriac, sent word of them to the Syrian Metropolitan, Athanasius Yeshue Samuel, at the Monastery of St. Mark in the Arab sector of Jerusalem.

The Arab-Israeli conflict was at its height at the time the Bedouin were trying to dispose of the scrolls. Jerusalem was divided into two armed camps, and communication between the two was almost impossible.

After much confusion and many mistakes the scrolls were sold by the Bedouin in two lots – one to Professor E. L. Sukenik of the Hebrew University, and the other to Metropolitan Samuel of St. Mark's Syrian Orthodox Monastery. It was a considerable time before either of these men knew of the collection which

THE AREA OF THE QUMRAN CAVES, in the Judean Wilderness about two miles west of the Dead Sea. Courtesy, Matson Photo Service.

A CAVE ENTRANCE at Qumran. Members of the Qumran Community lived in the caves and carried on their communal activities in the Community Center nearby. Courtesy, Photo Leon, Jerusalem.

AIR VIEW OF KHIRBET QUMRAN, indicating the plan of the settlement. Courtesy, Palestine Archaeological Museum.

the other had purchased, although Metropolitan Samuel knew that he had been unable to secure the entire group of manuscripts which the Bedouin were attempting to sell. Metropolitan Samuel brought the scrolls which were in his possession to the United States, but was unable to find a buyer here. Then, through a third party, he sold the scrolls to the State of Israel. All of the scrolls from the initial find at Cave 1 are now together in a magnificent structure known as the Shrine of the Book adjacent to the Hebrew University, Jerusalem.

The initial finds at Cave 1 included a scroll giving the greater part of the book of the prophet Isaiah, formerly called "St. Mark's Isaiah Scroll." With the discovery of other documents at other caves in the area, a new method of notation was devised so that the first Isaiah scroll is now described as 1Q Isa[a] (meaning: Cave 1, Qumran, first Isaiah scroll). This first Isaiah scroll, together with a commentary on the first two chapters of the Biblical book of Habakkuk and a sectarian document called the Manual of Discipline, also from the first finds at Cave 1, were published in 1950-51 by the American Schools of Oriental Research.

Scholars from the American Schools of Oriental Research had been of help to Metropolitan Samuel in identifying the scrolls which he had purchased from the Bedouin, and in estimating their age. Since it was felt that the value of the scrolls would be enhanced if the world of scholarship could study them, the Metropolitan gave permission to photograph and publish the ancient texts.

A second Isaiah scroll (1Q Isa[b]), a group of thanksgiving psalms (called by their Hebrew name "Hodayoth") and a scroll called "The War between the Children of Light and the Children of Darkness" from its first line (or simply the "War Scroll," 1Q M) were published by the Bialik Foundation and the Hebrew University (1948, 1950, and 1955). A work which was earlier thought to be an apocryphal book, Lamech, was identified as an Aramaic midrash on Genesis. The difficulty of unrolling this poorly preserved scroll made it the last of the manuscripts from Cave 1 to be studied. It was published by the Hebrew University in 1956 with the title, "A Genesis Apocryphon."

After the first scrolls were in the hands of competent scholars there followed a period of lively discussion and controversy concerning the origin and dating of the scrolls. This discussion formed a prelude to archeological work at the reputed site of the manuscript find. Early in 1949, G. Lankester Harding, then director of Antiquities of the Kingdom of Jordan, and Father Roland de Vaux of the Dominican Ècole Biblique visited and excavated the manuscript cave (now Cave 1). What they found proved that the claim that the scrolls had been discovered there was correct. In the cave they found manuscript fragments, linen wrappings, fragments of jars, Roman lamps, and Roman cooking pot fragments. This helped them to reconstruct the history of the cave. The excavation of the ruin (*khirbe* is the name archaeologists give to a ruin) nearby, known as Khirbet Qumran, was also to provide important material for a scholarly reconstruction of the life of the community that produced the scrolls.

IV. Other Qumran Caves

Both inexperienced Bedouin in search for "treasure" (or the *baksheesh* or "handouts of money," which a find will bring) and experienced archaeologists continued the search for manuscripts. The results were not disappointing. A second cave (Cave 2) yielded about one hundred fragments of the books of Exodus, Leviticus, Numbers, Deuteronomy, Jeremiah, Psalms, and Ruth. Dampness, worms, and rats have had their way with these precious manuscripts, but scholars do not despise even the fragment. Cave 3 produced the now famous copper scroll with its suggestion of buried treasure (which archaeologists do not take seriously). This scroll was sawed into strips at the university in Manchester, England, and subsequently published.

Next in importance to Cave 1 is the fourth manuscript-bearing cave. Literally tens of thousands of manuscript scraps were found in Cave 4, providing what Professor Frank Cross calls "the ultimate in jig-saw puzzles" as the scholar seeks to piece them together in their proper order and relationship. Among the ninety Bible manuscripts identified from Cave 4 every book of the Old Testament except Esther is represented. Thirteen manuscripts of Deuteronomy, twelve of Isaiah, ten of the Psalms, and numerous manuscripts of other Old Testament books have been identified. There is a well-preserved manuscript of the Books of Samuel with a papyrus backing which was placed there in antiquity. Apocryphal books, commentaries on Old Testament books, astronomical and cryptical writings are among the hundreds of Cave 4 texts now in the process of publication by the Oxford University Press.

Eleven caves have produced at least four hundred manuscripts to date. Reports of other discoveries in the Qumran area reach us from time to time. It is encouraging to know that careful scholars are devoting their energies to the reading, identification, and editing of these texts.

V. Wadi Murabba'at

Our discussion of the Dead Sea Scrolls centers around those finds which were made in the proximity of Khirbet Qumran. The caves in that area give evidence that they are related to Qumran history. In the search for manuscripts which the discoveries in the Qumran caves set off, other areas were explored and other, unrelated, finds have been made. Were it not for the sensational finds in the Qumran area, these other discoveries would have been widely publicized. As it is, they are not widely known, except among scholars. However, we cannot overlook them entirely in this discussion.

About twelve miles south of Qumran, in a remote part of the country southeast of Bethlehem, four manuscript-bearing caves have been found. As in the case of the Qumran caves, Bedouin brought the first finds to the attention of would-be purchasers. Father de Vaux, in company with the Director of the Department of Antiquities, was able to arrange with the Bedouin to visit the area where the manuscripts were found. In January and February 1952 the caves were excavated.

Authorities date the manuscripts from Wadi Murabba'at in the second century A.D. A variety of papyrus and sheep-skin material has been found. Letters from "Simeon ben Kosibah," identified as Bar Kochba, the leader of the second Jewish revolt, have stirred considerable discussion. Coins from the time of the second Jewish revolt are cited as proof for the second century dating of the scrolls. Among Biblical scrolls, a copy of the Minor Prophets (Joel-Zechariah) may be singled out as important, as it is closely related to the traditional, Masoretic text. Fragments of four leather scrolls – one of Genesis, two of Exodus, and one of Deuteronomy – show signs of having been violently torn up. Perhaps this was the work of the Roman soldiers who put down the revolt.

VI. Khirbet al-Mird

Northeast of the famous Mar Saba Monastery in a cave in the Wadi en-Nar, the southwestern continuation of the Kedron Valley, the Bedouin found manuscript material which scholars date from the fifth to the eighth centuries A.D. The area was

ARCHAEOLOGIST YIGAEL YADIN examines Bar Kochba letters from the time of the Second Jewish Revolt (A.D. 132-135). Courtesy, Israel Office of Information.

LETTER OF JOSHUA BEN GILGULA, chief of the Jewish insurgents at Murabba'at, containing a hint of the approach of the Roman army at the time of the Second Jewish Revolt (A.D. 132-135). Courtesy, Palestine Archaeological Museum.

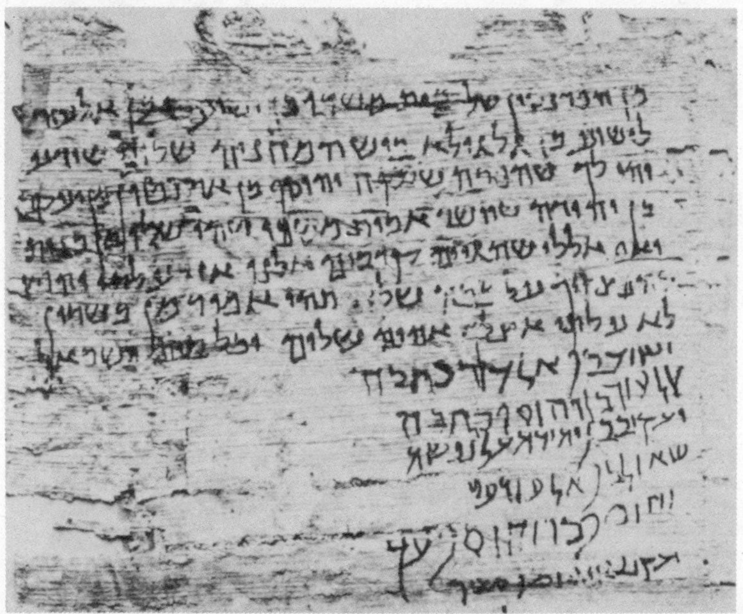

explored in February and March 1953 by a Belgian expedition. Arabic, Greek, and Syriac documents were found, including fragments of Biblical codices, all dating from the late Byzantine and early Arabic periods. They were related neither to the Qumran nor the Murabba'at finds, but will be of interest to students of the later periods. The Biblical fragments from Khirbet al-Mird are of Christian origin, whereas those of Qumran and Murabba'at belonged to the Jews.

2

KHIRBET QUMRAN

It was to be expected that excavations at the Khirbet Qumran should follow the discovery of scrolls in nearby caves. The Qumran ruin (Khirbet Qumran) had been noted by travellers for years. It is located on a northern terrace of the Wadi Qumran, twelve hundred yards from the Dead Sea.

In 1857, Feleceen de Saulcy, describing his travels in the Dead Sea area, identified Qumran as the site of ancient Gomorrah. This view has since been completely discredited both on geographical and linguistic criteria. Gomorrah was situated at the southern end of the Dead Sea, and Qumran is near the northwest corner of the sea. Linguistically there is no resemblance to Gomorrah in the name Qumran.

The German orientalist, Gustav Dalman, reasoned that the ruins of Qumran, with the cemetery nearby, must have been a Roman military outpost. While this guess was not to prove correct in detail, evidence does indicate that, for a short time, the tenth Roman legion did occupy it.

I. Excavation

A preliminary investigation of the ruin in 1949 by G. Lankester Harding and Father de Vaux proved inconclusive, but serious work began in November 1951 under the auspices of the Jordan Department of Antiquities, the Archaeological Museum of Palestine, and the Ècole Biblique. It was quickly determined that the site was occupied by the people who used the caves, and that the cemetery nearby was contemporaneous with the site.

Further excavations in 1953 and 1954 enable us to reconstruct the life of the members of the Qumran community with remarkable reality. A rectangular community center, 30 x 37 meters in size, built of large undressed stones with mud plaster, was the nucleus of the building complex. A massive tower at the northwest corner was used for defense. East of the tower was a kitchen with several fireplaces, and southwest of the tower were assembly rooms or refectories for the community. At the east is a large room which at first puzzled the excavators. When the archaeologists pieced together fragments of a plaster table and bench and discovered two inkwells (one bronze, one terra cotta), they concluded that this was the scriptorium, or writing room. One of the inkwells actually contained dried ink! Here many of the scrolls found in near-by caves must have been produced.

Southeast of the main building two cisterns, several large sinks, and a latrine with a kind of "septic tank" were found. Water, collected in the natural reservoirs at the base of the cliffs, was

RUINS OF QUMRAN with the Dead Sea and the mountains of ancient Moab (Modern Jordan) in the distance. Courtesy, Photo Leon, Jerusalem.

THE DOMESTIC QUARTER of the Qumran Community, showing the mill for grinding grain. Courtesy, Palestine Archaeological Museum.

channeled by means of a stone aqueduct to the intricate system of reservoirs which served such an important function in the Qumran community. Not only was it necessary to provide for normal needs of water but also the ceremonial washings which provided ritual purity for the members of the community.

The stairs, cistern floor, and several rooms of the ruin give conclusive evidence of a disasterous earthquake. Father de Vaux and others feel that the clearly definable cracks at Khirbet Qumran date to the year 31 B.C. Josephus described an earthquake which shook Judea in that year.

Father de Vaux has also excavated about twenty graves in various parts of the cemetery. Female as well as male skeletons have been identified. The absence of jewelry and ornamental objects indicates that this community practiced a monastic discipline which did not allow such finery.

II. History

Pottery and coins have enabled the excavator to assign exact dates for the settlement of Khirbet Qumran. Present indications are that the site was occupied in three periods, with some evidence of sporadic occupation at other times. It has been suggested, on the basis of the archaeological evidence, that the settlement was built in the days of Alexander Jannaeus (110 B.C.) and occupied until the earthquake of 31 B.C. Then the tower was ruined, the pool was cracked, and the entire area was rendered useless. The area was presumably abandoned at that time.

In the time of Archelaus (4 B.C.-A.D. 6) the Qumran area was re-occupied. Extensive repairs were made and the community center was enlarged. The evidence indicates that this second occupation was by the group that had occupied it before the earthquake. About A.D. 68, however, the settlement came to an end. Roman armies were bent on humbling the Jews who had dared to defy them. The Qumran community hid its precious manuscripts in nearby caves – perhaps with the thought that they would return, when the clouds of war had lifted, and continue their monastic life. However, they never returned. While some of these caves were doubtless discovered in antiquity, others remained undisturbed by human hands until the mid-twentieth century.

There is evidence that Roman soldiers occupied Khirbet Qumran after A.D. 68. Their presence, however, contributed nothing to its history.

It is now clear that the caves, cemetery and community center (Khirbet Qumran) are related. The people who lived in the caves and carried on their communal activities in the community center were the ones who copied the manuscripts found in the caves, and hid them there when they saw that their community was going to be destroyed by the approaching Roman legion.

3

THE DATE OF THE SCROLLS

After the finding of the first scrolls had become public knowledge, the enthusiasm of those associated with the American Schools of Oriental Research set the stage for a "battle of the scrolls." Able and experienced scholars in varied fields became champions of contradictory theories of date and authorship. The mystery which surrounded the finding of the scrolls, and the contradictory stories of those who first presented them to the scholarly world provided fuel for the fire of controversy.

The enthusiasm of W. F. Albright of Johns Hopkins University, one of America's foremost scholars in the field of Biblical Archaeology, is typical of the reception given the scrolls. Writing to John C. Trever at the American Schools, in Jerusalem, he said, "My heartiest congratulations on the greatest manuscript discovery of modern times! There is no doubt in my mind that the script is more archaic than that of the Nash Papyrus . . . I would prefer a date around 100 B.C. . . . What an absolutely incredible find! And there can happily not be the slightest doubt in the world about the genuineness of the manuscript."

Yet it was not long before doubt was expressed! Solomon Zeitlin, Professor of Rabbinic Literature at Dropsie College, Philadelphia, was convinced that the scrolls were of medieval origin and that the world of modern Semitic scholarship had become the victim of a gigantic hoax similar to the Piltdown hoax in the science of anthropology. Largely from internal evidence, a school of thought arose which challenged the conclusions of the scholars associated with the American Schools of Oriental Research.

The question concerning the date of the Qumran scrolls involves a series of other questions. We would like to know when the non-Biblical texts found at Qumran were composed. The compositions may be dated long before the dates of our copies. The contents of each document have been studied carefully but scholars will continue to wrestle with historical and linguistic problems for years to come.

As far as possible, we would like to determine when each of the manuscripts – Biblical and non-Biblical – was copied. Certain of the manuscripts may antedate others by centuries. Some of the scrolls may have been brought to Qumran at the time of the establishment of the community. Others were certainly produced in the scriptorium which has been discovered in the ruins of Khirbet Qumran. A study of the writing and the materials used by the scribes has provided some clues concerning the time when the scrolls were produced. It would also be helpful to know when, and under what circumstances the scrolls were deposited in the caves. The late E. L. Sukenik suggested that the scrolls were buried in the caves because they were worn out or defective and thus not fit to keep in circulation. We know that the Jews disposed of such texts in a repository called a "Genizeh." It was from such a genizeh that the Zadokite fragment was found in the city of Cairo in the late nineteenth century – a document which has close affinities with the Qumran texts.

Most scholars, however, are of the opinion that the Qumran texts were placed in their caves by members of the community who wished them to be preserved from the Roman legions which were preparing for the siege of Jewish strongholds, including Jerusalem, in the years preceding A.D. 70. In this matter, as in other areas of inquiry, the testimony of the archaeologist is decisive.

I. Palaeography

By palaeography we mean the study or science of deciphering ancient writings, determining their origin and period of history. The Qumran texts did not present problems of decipherment (save in the instance of a text written in code) but they did challenge scholars to try to determine the period during which the letters of the alphabet were written in the forms in which they appear in the scrolls.

The phenomena dealt with by palaeography is complicated. Styles of writing change, and it is usually possible to note the direction of these changes, and to determine that a letter written in a given way was written at a specific time. Yet archaizing tendencies must be reckoned with. On formal occasions we make use of "Old English" script. Our desire to be quaint may result in using "Ye" as the spelling of the definite article.

Archaizing tendencies did exist in ancient Israel. This was noticeably true during the Maccabean period with its aversion to things foreign and emphasis on things Jewish. In the Habakkuk Commentary from Cave 1, Qumran, the sacred name of Yahweh – the tetragrammaton – is written in early Hebrew script. This is doubtless an archaizing due to regard for the sacredness of the Divine Name.

A. Early Hebrew Inscriptions.

In discussing the history of the Hebrew alphabet, scholars distinguish two types of letters. The term "early Hebrew" (or "archaic Hebrew") is used to designate the script of the pre-exilic period, that is, before the sixth century B.C. The most ancient example of early Hebrew writing is the so-called Gezer calendar, belonging probably to the age of Saul or David (eleventh century B.C.). The Gezer calendar is a limestone plaque describing the activities of a Palestinian farmer throughout the year.

About eighty pieces of broken pottery with inscriptions in ink (known as ostraca) found at Samaria provide us with examples of "early Hebrew" writing in the dialect of Israel. Most of these ostraca were invoices for oil and wine paid to the king's official at Samaria. They are dated about the middle of the ninth century B.C.

In 1880 the Siloam inscription was found carved in the wall of an aqueduct, to commemorate the completion of the building of the aqueduct. It is dated in the time of Hezekiah (700 B.C.).

Remnants of a large collection of correspondence and other documents from the city of Lachish were discovered in the year 1935, with an additional discovery of three ostraca in 1938. These letters were written immediately before the destruction of the city, in the time of Nebuchadnezzar, and afford us a picture of the last hours of independence in the cities of Judah in the early months of 587 B.C.

Further examples of early Hebrew writing have been found in the mounds of southern Palestine. Jar handles, stone seals, and inscribed weights and measures have provided examples of the script of the pre-exilic period.

A RECONSTRUCTED SCROLL JAR, with other pottery and coins discovered at Qumran. Courtesy, Palestine Archaeological Museum.

B. "Square" Alphabet.

During the Babylonian exile the "square script" based on the Aramaic alphabet and strongly influenced by the early Hebrew alphabet became the usual means of written expression. A sepulchral inscription from 'Araq el-Emir, southeast of Es-Salt, Jordan, is considered a transition script from the early Hebrew to the square Hebrew. Albright dates this inscription at 400 B.C. Meisler suggests a date in the late sixth or early fifth century B.C.

Square Hebrew inscriptions have been found on Palestinian ossuaries (depositories for the bones of the dead) from the time of the Maccabees. A few tomb monuments and ancient synagogue inscriptions give further samples of the script.

When John Trever first examined the scrolls in the possession of Metropolitan Samuel he compared their script with that of the Nash Papyrus, a fragment containing the ten commandments and the Shema (Deuteronomy 6:1-2), which has been variously dated. Solomon Birnbaum suggests an early second century B.C. date; Albright holds to a date in the Maccabean age (165 B.C.-37 B.C.). F. C. Burkitt and S. A. Cook prefer dates in the first and second centuries, A.D., respectively. Millar Burrows is of the opinion that the Isaiah Scroll (1QIsa[a]), the Manual of Discipline, and the Nash Papyrus belong to the same half or three-quarters of a century.

In the discussion of palaeography scholars make use of Aramaic as well as Hebrew writing because of the fact that both use the "square script." Third century B.C. Aramaic papyri found at Edfu on the upper Nile exhibit a form of the square script that is definitely more archaic than that of the Qumran scrolls. The fifth century B.C. Aramaic papyri found at Assuan (ancient Elephantine) exhibit a very early form of the square writing and were certainly written long before the Qumran scrolls.

The evidence from palaeography clearly dates the majority of the Qumran scrolls in the period of the Nash Papyrus which has been dated by competent scholars in the period between 200 B.C. and A.D. 200. Other evidence will help to establish a more exact date for the period of the scrolls.

Palaeography is challenged particularly by a fragment of the Book of Leviticus written in the early Hebrew script. Solomon A. Birnbaum suggested that this fragment dates back to the fifth century B.C. The Leviticus fragment may be our oldest Biblical portion in manuscript. It is worth noting that the text of this fragment is identical with the Masoretic text.

THE POTTER'S KILN, Qumran. Courtesy, Palestine Archaeological Museum.

All writers do not agree with Birnbaum, however. Some suggest that the use of the early Hebrew script is an example of the tendency to archaize, which is illustrated by similar script on Maccabean coins and the writing of the tetragrammaton in the early script in the Habakkuk commentary. Burrows suggests that the fragments must be dated between the fifth and the first centuries B.C. with preference given to the earlier half of the period.

II. Archaeology

The discovery of the Qumran scrolls was clouded with an air of mystery. One of the earliest reports indicated that they had been in the Syrian monastery library for some time. The attempt of Metropolitan Samuel to sell them at a price which seemed exorbitant added to the desire on the part of many to debunk the reported find in a cave near the Dead Sea. Solomon Zeitlin was sure they had been taken from a synagogue at Hebron during Arab-Israeli riots.

POTTERY discovered at the site of the pantry which served the Qumran Community. Courtesy, Palestine Archaeological Museum.

A salutary effect of the "battle of the scrolls" was the serious effort made by competent scholars to use every means at their disposal to test the stories of the Arabs and the claims of the scholars who first examined the scrolls. If this was at times tedious, the results were not un-rewarding.

When archaeologists were able to visit the site of Cave 1, where the first manuscripts were found, doubts concerning the truthfulness of the Bedouin's story were quickly dispelled. Hundreds of bits of manuscript were found. Potsherds, fragments of cloth which had originally bound the manuscripts, and pottery provided material with which the archaeologist could verify earlier reports and estimate the date of the manuscripts. It was thought at first that the pottery was of the late Hellenistic period, but later excavations at the nearby Khirbet Qumran turned up similar pottery in the same strata with coins attesting an occupation from the reign of Augustus (31 B.C.-A.D. 14) to the first Jewish revolt (66-70 A.D.).

The fact that the Bedouin claimed to have found the scrolls

in jars has lent particular significance to the attempt to date the pottery. While the jars and the scrolls need not have been produced at the same time, it is reasonable to suppose that the dating of the jars would furnish a clue to the period in which the scrolls were produced, or, at least, the period during which they were hidden in the caves.

The story of the finding of the scrolls in jars has an interesting Biblical parallel. Jeremiah the prophet was so confident of the fulfillment of God's promise to restore Israel to its own land after the Babylonian captivity, that he purchased a field in Anathoth, near Jerusalem. Documents were drawn up as "evidence of purchase" and Jeremiah was commanded to put the title deeds to his property "in an earthen vessel, that they may continue many days" (Jeremiah 32:14).

Three of the jars which contained Qumran scrolls are now in the United States. The first to come to this country is in the Oriental Institute of the University of Chicago. The others are in the Zion Research Library, Boston, Massachusetts, and the Walters Art Gallery, Baltimore, Maryland.

Although the Qumran community never returned to claim its hidden writings, such an experience is related in II Maccabees. We are told that Judas the Maccabee gathered together the writings which had been scattered as a result of war (2:14). He adds, "And they are still with us." There is, of course, no reference to scrolls placed in jars and hidden in caves in this reference to the wars of the Maccabees. There is, however, the historical note that in a time of war precious books are apt to be scattered. The Qumran community attempted to prevent this by secreting its library in nearby caves.

The badly decomposed cloth which was found in Cave 1 was carefully studied by experts in the field of ancient textiles. A microscopic examination proved that the cloth was linen. It was also determined that the linen was of native Palestinian manufacture, and ancient. Nothing more could be determined concerning the date of the cloth from examination. It was to bear witness concerning the antiquity of the scrolls from another type of study.

III. Carbon 14

The discovery of the Carbon 14 method of dating organic matter has been heralded as "one of the most remarkable scientific accomplishments of the decade." Willard F. Libby was a nuclear chemist at the University of Chicago when, in 1947 –

the same year the Qumran scrolls were discovered – he announced the discovery of a method of determining the age of organic matter by measuring the loss of radioactive carbon.

Carbon 14 is an unstable (radioactive) heavy form of carbon with an atomic weight of 14. Normal, stable carbon has an atomic weight of 12. The "half-life" of Carbon 14 is around 5,500 years. This means that an ounce of Carbon 14 is reduced to one-half ounce in 5,500 years; half the remainder decays in the next 5,500 years, and so on. By measuring the Carbon 14 in organic matter Mr. Libby found a means of determining the age of living things that lived during the past 25,000 years.

The scientific validity of Libby's method was demonstrated by testing organic material of known date, such as a piece of wood from the boat of a Pharaoh of Egypt who is known to have lived 3,750 years ago, and a piece of the corewood of a sequoia tree with exactly 2,905 rings marking annual growth. In each case the dates obtained by the Carbon 14 test were correct within the 5% to 10% margin of error. Libby was awarded the 1951 Research Corporation award for "one of the greatest contributions of the century to archaeology."

Since the Carbon 14 method involves burning the material tested it was not possible to test the scrolls directly. It seemed wise, however, to sacrifice some of the linen wrappings in order to get a Carbon 14 reading on their date. Cloth from the scroll wrapping was brought to America by Professor J. L. Kelso, and arrangements were made through Carl H. Kraeling to have Libby make the required test. The result was made known in January 1951 when Libby wrote, "We have completed a measurement on the linen wrappings from the Dead Sea Scrolls which you furnished us on November 14, 1950 . . . The date obtained is 1917 plus or minus 200 years, or 33 A.D. plus or minus 200." According to this criteria, the linen wrapping of the scrolls dates from 168 B.C. to A.D. 233, or somewhere during the period from Antiochus Epiphanes to Origen. The linen wrapping may, of course, date from a period either earlier or later than that during which the scrolls were written. If the linen wrappings were made for the scrolls, the presumption would be that the scrolls antedate the wrappings. In any case it is significant that the Carbon 14 test agrees with the conclusions reached by palaeography and archaeology.

IV. Internal Evidence

A small number of scholars challenged the validity of the methods of dating the scrolls based on palaeography. They claimed that there was not sufficient inscribed material in the pre-Christian period to justify making positive identification. They considered that the Carbon 14 method of dating was still in the experimental stage and repudiated any dates determined by its tests. Since scrolls were not actually found in the jars, Solomon Zeitlin insisted that "there is no evidence that the scrolls were ever stored in these jars." In fact he considered the archaeological evidence as irrelevant and maintained that internal considerations alone could establish the dating of the scrolls. This internal evidence, particularly in the area of vocabulary and spelling, he considered conclusive in pointing to a medieval date for the scrolls. Most of the questions concerning the antiquity of the scrolls have been answered, but Solomon Zeitlin remains unconvinced. He assures us that Jews did not write commentaries on the Bible in antiquity. Since Hebrew was a living language, he asserts that commentaries were unnecessary. This argument is certainly valid in the area of historical-grammatical-critical commentaries such as the modern Bible student uses in order to reconstruct the Biblical situation. Removed by language, time, and geography we need commentaries in a sense in which a Jew living in Palestine in antiquity did not need them.

It should be pointed out, however, that the Habakkuk Commentary from Cave 1, Qumran is not a commentary in the modern sense of the term. It is related to the ancient Jewish Midrashic literature. The interpretation (Hebrew, *pesher*) applies a passage of Scripture to a historical situation at the time of the composition of the commentary. This is analogous to the way in which well-meaning Bible students of a generation ago saw Hitler or Mussolini in the prophetic portions of Daniel and Revelation. In the Habakkuk Commentary the prophecies were considered fulfilled in the "Teacher of Righteousness" and his enemy the "Wicked Priest" – elusive characters to us, but clearly identified in the minds of members of the Qumran community. In some cases, at least, the commentary was considered authoritative by the Qumran community. In no case is the grammar or historical context of Scripture explained, as if to enlighten someone removed in language, time, or geography from the Biblical world.

Much is made of arguments from vocabulary in the writings of Zeitlin. He insists that expressions like "the teacher of righteousness" were not used before the middle ages. Their presence in the Qumran sectarian writings is used as an argument for a late date of the scrolls. The Jewish sect of the Karaites, in particular, is held responsible for the origin of much of the terminology which we meet in the Qumran literature.

Yet it is possible to reason in circles in a matter such as this. If terminology is used in the Qumran documents and in Karaite literature it is the province of scholarship to determine the relationship, if any, between the Qumran community and the Karaites. While, in the absence of other evidence, it is conceivable that the two groups are identical, the preponderance of other evidence indicates an ancient date for the scrolls. In no study of literature can we arbitrarily fix a date when a word or expression was first used. Such dates are always tentative, and additional information must be used to correct earlier conclusions when necessary.

While there are problems associated with a pre-A.D. 70 dating of the scrolls, the evidence of palaeography and archaeology, with the added witness of Carbon 14 dating present strong testimony to a date in that early period. Internal evidence is in harmony with such a conclusion, as will be noted by a study of the scrolls themselves.

4

THE HISTORICAL BACKGROUND

During the pre-exilic period Israel was faced constantly with the temptation to adopt a creed and cult based on the ideas of its Canaanite neighbors. The prophets attempted to resist the tide of Baalism and call the people back to the worship of Yahweh. A deep-rooted tendency to idolatry continued, however, right up to the time of the captivity of the southern kingdom in Babylon.

The exile, although considered a divine punishment inflicted upon the people because of their sins, issued in much that was good. Banished from land and temple, the study of the law (the sacred Scriptures) became a burning passion. While some settled down in Babylon and prospered there, others seized the opportunity to return — which was made possible by the decree of Cyrus. The pilgrims who returned to Zion during the Persian period (549-331 B.C.) were few in number, poor in material resources, but strong in faith and in the determination to keep themselves and their faith pure from any "foreign" elements. While this attitude antagonized possible friendly neighbors, it was necessary to guarantee the purity of Jewish life and worship.

I. Alexander the Great

However, a new figure soon appeared on the horizon. Alexander the Great, in the words of W. W. Tarn, "so changed the world [that] nothing after him could be as it was before." If idolatry had been the stumbling block in the pre-exilic period, Hellenism was the great post-exilic temptation. A third century B.C. writer has summarized the issues: "In recent times, under the foreign rule of the Persians, and then of the Macedonians, by whom the Persian empire was overthrown, intercourse with other races had led to many of the traditional Jewish ordinances losing their hold."

Alexander was more than a power-mad despot. A pupil of the philosopher Aristotle, he was thoroughly convinced that Greek culture was the one force which could unify the world. Conquering the Near East as far as the Punjab region of India, he determined to found a new city in each country of his empire which would be a model for the re-ordering of the urban life of the country as a whole along Greek lines. Materially speaking this meant the erection of fine public buildings, a gymnasium for games, an open air theatre and everything that would simulate life in a Greek city-state. Individuals were encouraged to take Greek names, adopt Greek dress and the Greek language – in short to become "Hellenised."

The material aspects of Hellenism must have seemed attractive to large segments of the population. Trade and commerce brought wealth to the new merchant class. Libraries and schools were welcomed by the scholars. Better housing and better food meant a standard of living which many had never dreamed possible. Many in Israel, as elsewhere, were glad to accept this veneer of Greek culture.

II. Alexander's Successor

At the age of 33, Alexander died in Babylon. For a number of years the future of the Near East was uncertain, but his generals succeeded in dividing the empire among themselves, and the tide of Hellenism increased. While the Ptolemies of Egypt and the Seleucids of Syria fought among themselves for land and power, they were in complete agreement concerning their social and cultural mission. The union of the world brought about by the propagation of Greek civilization was no mean goal.

III. Reaction in Israel

Some Jews were ready to adopt Hellenism. They took Greek names, accepted a school of Greek philosophy in addition to their Jewish faith, and tried to combine the wisdom of Greece with the faith of Israel.

Others however met Hellenism with a spirit of resistance. For example, the Hasidim held firmly to all of the principles and regulations of the law and met the challenge of Hellenism by devoting themselves more conscientiously to the study of Scripture.

IV. Antiochus Epiphanes

By the time Antiochus IV (Epiphanes) came to the throne of Syria the situation in Palestine had reached the breaking point. A considerable party of Jews was favorable to Hellenism and was ready to welcome "reforms" in that direction. Antiochus was having trouble with the rival kingdom of the Ptolemies to the south, and needed money to prosecute his war.

We are told in II Maccabees how a certain Jason, whose political sympathies were with Syria, had supplanted his pro-Egyptian brother Onias III as High Priest by the simple expedient of paying well for the office. To Antiochus this was a matter of practical politics, and he could not understand the shock of the Hasidim at the sale of the priestly office. The pious in Israel were shocked even more when, three years later, a man named Menelaus who was not even of the high priestly family offered a higher price for the office, and got it.

Jason was not ready to surrender the priestly and political functions of his office without a fight. When Antiochus was busy in Egypt, Jason rallied his supporters and massacred the followers of Menelaus. To Antiochus this was sheer treason. He returned to Jerusalem, confirmed Menelaus in his office, and showed his contempt for the Jews by desecrating and despoiling the Temple.

The next few years witnessed a wave of anti-Semitism unparalleled until recent times. By order of Antiochus, the Mosaic law was annulled and its ordinances – circumcision, the sabbath, and sacrifice – were proscribed under penalty of death. Heathen altars were set up throughout the land. A statue of Zeus Olympios was set up in the Holy Place of the Temple, and the worship of the God of Israel was outlawed.

V. The Maccabean Revolt

The response of the Jews was varied. Some willingly yielded. Some quietly hoped and prayed for divine intervention. Some fought.

In the little village of Modin, about thirteen miles west of Bethel, an officer of Antiochus attempted to enforce apostasy at a pagan altar which he had erected. The village priest, Mattathias, was given the first opportunity to sacrifice, thus showing his loyalty to the king. He refused to do so. Thereupon a frightened Jew came forward in order to perform the required rite. Mattathias then stepped out, and killed both the apostate Jew and the officer of Antiochus.

Aged Mattathias and his five sons, joined by many of the Hasidim, fled to the hill country northwest of Jerusalem where they waged guerilla warfare with the Syrian armies. Four Syrian armies were defeated in two years. When Mattathias died, Judas became leader. After three years of desecration the Temple was cleansed and the daily sacrifices restored (December 25, 165 B.C.). The Jewish feast of Hanukkah celebrates the cleansing of the Temple by Judas.

Judas, his brothers, and their successors ruled Palestine for about a century. After securing religious liberty they pressed on, determined to secure full political independence. A dynasty, first of ruling High Priests, and then of kings, governed the Jews until the Romans added Judea to their domain.

VI. The Hasidim

In I Maccabees 2:41 we read of a group of "mighty men of Israel . . . such as were voluntarily devoted to the law" who joined Mattathias and his followers in resisting the attempts of Antiochus to enforce Hellenism upon the Jews. This party is known as the *Hasidim,* from a Hebrew word meaning "pious." They are otherwise termed Hasideans or Assideans in our history books.

The Hasidim were interested in securing religious liberty for Israel but they had no love for Jewish nationalism. Because Judas Maccabeus was not "of the seed of Aaron" they supported Alcimus (Hebrew, Eliakim) for the office of High Priest, but they were disillusioned by his subsequent cruelty. The Syrians offered them assurance of religious freedom and they were happy to accept the offer. They refused to cooperate with the Hasmonaeans (the successors of Judas the Maccabee) in their fight for political independence.

Although the name Hasidim died out following the Maccabean struggle, their historical continuity has been traced in later Jewish life. Certain of their tenets and ideals lived on in the best elements of the Pharisaic party, and they have been considered forerunners of the Essenes, who were also known for their strict legal observance. The name "Pharisee" comes from a word which conveys the meaning of a separatist, a non-conformist. Some scholars suggest that the terms Hasid (singular of Hasidim) and Essene are both derived from a word with the meaning of pious.

VII. The Jewish Sects

During the reign of John Hyrcanus (134-104 B.C.), a son of the last of the sons of Mattathias, we read for the first time of a religious party which was to leave its mark upon the subsequent history of Judaism. John Hyrcanus was a Pharisee. Showing his friendship for his fellow-Pharisees he gave a great feast during which he expressed his desire "to do all things whereby he might please God and them." To prove his sincerity Hyrcanus asked "if they observed him offending in any point and going out of the right way, that they would call him back and correct him." Although the Pharisees as a group expressed their satisfaction with Hyrcanus, one of them (named Eleazar according to Josephus, or Judah, according to another version of the story) replied, "Since thou desirest to know the truth, if thou wilt be righteous in earnest, lay down the High-priesthood and content thyself with the civil government of the people." Hyrcanus was angered at this retort, and the Pharisees themselves appeared resentful. Josephus tells us that a Sadducee named Jonathan, taking advantage of the embarrassment of the Pharisees, suggested that Hyrcanus would soon know the attitude of the Pharisees toward him if they were asked to advise Hyrcanus concerning suitable punishment for the offender. When they suggested a "moderate punishment of stripes, but not of death," Hyrcanus felt that the insult represented the viewpoint of the Pharisees as a group, and he broke off friendly relations with them.

To what extent the story is to be regarded as true we may not say, but it does indicate the antagonism between Pharisees and Sadducees during this period. It also illustrates the growing antipathy between the Pharisees and the Hasmonean leaders. It has been suggested that the outspoken Pharisee who incurred the wrath of Hyrcanus may have broken with the party, extremist that he was, becoming the leader of the Essenes.

A. Pharisees.

Quoting Nicholas of Damascus, Josephus gives us a brief description of the Pharisees as observed by an outsider: ". . . a body of Jews who profess to be more religious than the others, and to explain the laws more exactly" (*Wars of the Jews*, i, 5:2).

While we are apt to think of the Pharisees as rigidly orthodox, in some respects they were the progressive element in Judaism. In order to meet new conditions, the Pharisees set about to reinterpret the law. The modification and adaptation of the law which resulted is known to us as "oral tradition." It will be remembered that Jesus condemned the attitude of placing the "tradition" or "commandments of men" above, or on a par with, the commandments of God contained in His Word. This oral tradition was later codified in the book called the Mishna. While accepted by later rabbinical Judaism it was rejected by the medieval Jewish sect of Karaites.

The developing and maintaining of the synagogue as a center of worship and instruction is largely an achievement of the Pharisees. They were generally admired by those Jews who were not committed to any Jewish sect.

B. Sadducees.

The Sadducees were largely an upper class party composed of the nobility of Jerusalem. The party was restricted to the high-priestly and aristocratic families. Historically the Sadducees had been friendly to the innovations of the Hellenistic party. Political interests tended to thrust religion into the background. Although claiming to believe the Old Testament (or, specifically, the Law) as authoritative, the Sadducees' orientation in theology was purely negative. He did not believe in spirits, angels, resurrection – or oral tradition. He kept aloof from the people. His sphere of influence was the Temple and its rites. The High-priesthood was in the hands of the Sadducees. The Pharisees claimed the authority of piety and learning; the Sadducees that of blood and position.

C. Zadokites.

A new term, "Zadokite," has entered the discussion of pre-Christian Judaism since the publication in 1910 of *Fragments of a Zadokite Work* discovered in 1896 in the *genizeh* of a Karaite synagogue in Cairo. Although the term Zadokite is analogous to the term Sadducee, it is certain that the groups had different historical developments. It has been suggested that a group of spiritually minded priests saw the drift of early second century B.C. Sadduceeism, separated from it and formed the nucleus of a new group. Whether this movement found spiritual affinity with an already existing group and imparted new life and vigor to it, or whether this particular group originated at this time is not clear.

We are told, in the *Zadokite Work,* that God looked with

favor on penitent Israel, "for with a perfect heart did they seek Him; and he raised for them a Teacher of Righteousness to lead them in the way of His heart and to make known to the last generations that which He would do to the last generations, the congregation of the faithless."

The Teacher of Righteousness had an enemy, for "there arose the man of scoffing who dripped to Israel (i.e. preached) waters of falsehood and cause them to go astray in a wilderness without way, by causing the pride of the world (or, eternal pride) to become low, by turning aside from the pathways of righteousness and by removing the landmark which the forefathers had set up in their inheritance, in order to cause the curses of His covenant to cleave to them, thus delivering them to the sword that shall execute the vengeance of the covenant."

Scholars are agreed that the *Zadokite Work* is related to the Qumran scrolls. Style, vocabulary, and allusions gave the first inkling of this fact. Discovery of copies of the *Zadokite Work* in Cave 6, Qumran, have confirmed the fact of historical relationship. The exact nature of the relationship (for there are differences in detail) is still obscure.

The *Zadokite Work* speaks of a group which was compelled to migrate to Damascus where, under the leadership of a leader called "the star" (cf. Numbers 24:17) they entered into a New Covenant (cf. Jeremiah 31:31) and organized a group which possessed characteristics which we would term monastic. A prominent leader of the sect is named the Teacher of Righteousness, a term which we meet again in the Qumran Habukkuk Commentary.

The date of the migration to Damascus mentioned in the *Zadokite Work* has been the subject of considerable discussion. Some have suggested that it was related to the removal of Onias III from his office as High Priest in the days of Antiochus Epiphanes. Charles Fritsch in *The Qumran Community* argues for a much later date. He suggests that the sojourn at Damascus took place during the reign of Herod the Great (37 B.C.–4 B.C.). Archaeological evidence indicates that the Qumran monastery was unoccupied at that time, and it appears to Fritsch a logical step to suggest that this is the period of the Damascus sojourn. The question seems to be: Did the Zadokites leave Jerusalem for Damascus (175 B.C.) and then migrate to Qumran? Did they go from Jerusalem to Qumran, then to Damascus, and then back to Qumran? A further possibility is that the so-called Damascus Covenanters joined forces with an already existing group of Qumran Covenanters.

One scholar, Rabinowitz, has advanced the view that the withdrawal from Judea to Damascus is but another way of describing the Babylonian captivity and the lessons learned "Beyond Damascus" by the faithful in Israel. While this view would solve some of the historical problems, the *Zadokite Work* does appear to discuss a historical migration to Damascus in days following the return from exile.

In any case evidence indicates that the Damascus Covenanters and the Qumran community are related (if not identical) and that a group of priests, "sons of Zadok," led a movement to which lay members were attracted. This movement had the name Zadokite applied to it because of its stress on its priestly legitimacy *vis-a-vis* the Jerusalem priesthood (which was corrupt in the eyes of the Zadokites). Zadok was High Priest under Solomon, and his descendants are regarded as the legitimate High Priests (Ezekiel 40:46).

D. Essenes.

Three ancient writers, Philo, Josephus, and Pliny, constitute our primary sources for a study of the Jewish sect of Essenes. The problem is somewhat complicated when we realize that the term Essene was used to describe groups which differed widely among themselves in important details. Pliny the Elder tells us that Essenes avoided women and refused to marry, whereas Josephus speaks of an order of marrying Essenes.

In seeking to explain his religion to the Greek-speaking world, Josephus spoke of three "Philosophies" – Pharisees, Sadducees, and Essenes. Evidently the term Essene was quite an elastic one, including various communities of Jews which were separatist in practice.

In general, ancient writers deal in a sympathetic way with the Essenes. Essenes lived lives of simplicity. They devoted much of their time to devotion and religious study. They were industrious. Each member was required to perform manual labor. They practiced community of goods and lived a life of strict discipline in submission to an overseer. The young were required to defer to the older members of the community. Those groups which renounced marriage adopted boys at an early age in order to inculcate and perpetuate the ideals of the movement. Slavery and war were repudiated. The Essenes did not take part in the Temple worship. The sources indicate that Essenes repudiated the idea of sacrifice, but the Zadokites simply repudiated the Jerusalem priesthood. They both differed from the Pharisees who continued to participate in Temple worship even though that worship was dominated by the Sadducees. We are told that the Essenes would not anoint their bodies with oil – a practice which they probably regarded as a "pampering of the flesh."

Numerically the Essenes were never large. Philo says there were four thousand of them. Pliny speaks of them as settled north of En Gedi (a probable reference to Khirbet Qumran), but we know they were also settled elsewhere. They inhabited many cities in Judea as well as many villages and populated areas. The virtue of hospitality was stressed, for we are told that members of the sect were welcomed in all of the Essene colonies.

Historically both Pharisees and Essenes stressed separation from defilement and the need of personal piety. They differed, however, in many details of doctrine and practice. Josephus tells us that, while the Essenes believed in immortality, they rejected the doctrine of bodily resurrection. The question of outside influences on Essenism is an interesting one, but we may note here that this denial of resurrection is probably to be related to the Greek philosophical concept of the evil of matter (nowhere taught in Scripture but frequently to be observed in ascetic movements). If matter is evil, and the body is material, then resurrection must logically be denied.

The Pharisees made it a rule that every man, at the age of eighteen, must take a wife. As we have observed, Essenes discouraged and, in some groups, forbade marriage. Pharisees took an active part in Jewish life, including the Temple services, but the Essenes formed a separate brotherhood. They deemed themselves the only true (i.e. pure) Israel, and refused to cooperate with what they believed to be the corrupt religious observances of their day.

E. Other Sects.

In the New Testament, and in the writings of Josephus we meet a sect known as the *Zealots*, a party of "home-rule" advocates who considered it an act of disloyalty to God to acknowledge Caesar as king. In contrast to the Pharisees, the Zealots refused to pay taxes. They harassed the Roman government and advocated the extremist measures which brought about the destruction of Jerusalem in A.D. 70.

The study of Judaism in the centuries immediately preceding and following the time of Christ presents a maze of small sects. Some accepted the claims of false Messiahs. Some advocated violence to establish an independent Israel. Some were pacifists and ascetics awaiting the fulfillment of Biblical prophecy.

5

THE SECTARIAN SCROLLS

Some may take exception to the use of the term "sectarian" to describe members of the Qumran community. The term conveys something of a stigma in modern usage. It is not so meant here. The term is used to distinguish those writings which were peculiar to the Qumran community, and, perhaps, related groups, from the Biblical texts found in the Qumran caves.

We use the term "normative Judaism" to describe that type of Judaism which has existed in an unbroken historical tradition from ancient times to the present. We meet it in the New Testament, in the Mishna and Talmud. The contemporary divisions of orthodox, conservative, and reformed Judaism trace their historical roots to this "normative Judaism." Since the party of the Sadducess ceased to exist after the destruction of the Temple (70 A.D.), "normative Judaism" is actually a continuation of the tradition of Pharisaic Judaism.

Normative Judaism regarded as sacred literature the books which make up our Old Testament. Apocryphal literature (including what scholars term the pseudepigrapha) was rejected. The Qumran community and those groups which related to it, made use of a body of literature in addition to the canonical Scriptures. Some of this literature consists of commentaries on Scripture. Other of it gives the rules of the community. Literature of this type has been designated "sectarian" to distinguish it from the literature which Qumran had in common with normative Judaism (i.e. the Scriptures). The large number of apocryphal writings discovered in the Qumran caves indicates the high regard in which such writings were held by the Qumran community. These, too, were rejected by normative Judaism.

The study of the sectarian scrolls is of value to students of history and language. The student of history desires to know the nature of pre-Christian Judaism. The period between the Testaments is not well documented. The Apocrypha, Josephus and other classical writers have helped us to write an inter-testamental history, but new light from literature written during this period is inestimable help in filling in the gaps.

It must be said, however, that nothing of a "revolutionary" nature has to this day emerged from a study of the scrolls. It is true that, if we are correct in identifying the Qumran community with the Essenes, we have a more vivid description of Essene life and dogma than we did previously. The importance of non-Pharisaic Judaism has taken on new meaning. The scrolls have enabled us to fill in our outlines of pre-Christian Judaism, but we have had no occasion to revise them.

One great benefit of the scrolls to the world of scholarship has resulted from a study of the vocabulary and grammar of the sectarian scrolls. Ideas expressed and the words chosen to illustrate them provide a helpful background for under-use of Hebrew in new contexts throws light on Old Testament vocabulary. The results of this type of study are never spectacular. They do, however, provide the basis for a scientific treatment of the Biblical text.

I. The Manual of Discipline

The scroll containing the Manual of Discipline has come to us in two fragments made up of five pieces of leather with a total length of over six feet. The height is about nine and one-half inches. There are eleven columns of text in this scroll but the beginning of the book has been lost. The Palestine Museum later recovered two additional columns which are thought to be related to the same manuscript as the Manual of Discipline. The lacunae (gaps) are considerable, and the relationship between the two portions cannot be defined with confidence. The eleven columns which were first discovered were published by the American Schools of Oriental Research in 1951 and the additional columns were published in 1955 in the book *Studies in the Judaean Desert: Qumran Cave I* by Bartholemy and Milik. We shall refer to them as the appendix to the Manual of Discipline.

Dupont-Sommer describes the Manual of Discipline as "a collection of various fragments, liturgical, legal, or moral in character, apparently arranged somewhat at random, without

TWO COLUMNS FROM THE MANUAL OF DISCIPLINE, one of the Cave 1 texts. Courtesy, Palestine Archaeological Museum.

any great logical order." The origin and early history of the book is unknown, but it seems to have been the book of principles which governed the Qumran community.

The so-called Zadokite work, published in 1910 by Solomon Schechter and known to have been related to the Qumran movement speaks of instruction "in the book of Hagu and in the teachings of the covenant" (10:6). Similarly the appendix to the Manual of Discipline (1:7) gives directions for instruction "in the book of Hagi" (or Hagu – the letters "i" and "u" cannot be distinguished in many of the Qumran scrolls. The letter "u" in Hebrew script is but a longer form of the same character which is used to represent "i").

The book of Hagu, according to Schechter, was "a regular set of rules of discipline for the initiation of novices and penitents." The relationship of the book of Hagu to the Manual of Discipline is one of those perplexing questions which give scholars much concern. Is the Manual of Discipline to be identified with the book of Hagu? It is interesting that the term which scholars used in describing the manual is practically identical to Schechter's conjecture as to the nature of the book of Hagu. If the Manual of Discipline is not to be identified with the book of Hagu it probably contains regulations based on that book.

The Manual of Discipline is our best source of information concerning pre-Christian sectarian Judaism. A study of its contents will help us to understand what the Qumran community thought of its own faithfulness to God and the unfaithfulness of other groups, both in and out of Judaism, which surrounded it. The ritual described in the Manual of Discipline indicates the way in which Old Testament Scripture was adapted to the needs of the sect and provides both comparisons and contrasts with later Christian usage.

A. Names by Which the Qumran Community Was Known.

We may gain an insight into the attitudes of the members of the Qumran community by an examination of the names which are used in the Manual of Discipline to describe the sect.

1. The Community (*Yaḥad*)

A term which occurs frequently in the Manual of Discipline is the Hebrew word *Yaḥad*. Scholars translate this word in terms of the community, the unity, and the union. This word is related to a verb meaning "to be united" and to the numeral one. This usage of the noun is, as far as we know, peculiar to the Qumran sect. The noun *Yaḥad* occurs once in the Bible (I Chronicles 12:17) in an expression which may be rendered literally, "I will have a heart toward you for unitedness" (*lᵉyaḥad*). Idiomatically the text might be rendered, "My heart shall be ready to become one with yours" (so Brown, Driver, and Briggs, *Lexicon*).

The term *Yaḥad* conveys something of the idea of the Greek *koinonia* which occurs frequently in the New Testament in the sense of communion or fellowship. Such social and economic concepts as marriage ties and business partnerships are described by this word.

Sectarian groups of all ages have made much of the sense of "belonging." Members of the Qumran community shared common property and a common life. Religious ties, based upon Scripture and the tenets particular to the sect produced a brotherhood which found a suitable name for itself in the term *yaḥad.*

2. The Party, Council (*'eṣah*)

As a noun meaning "counsel," or "advice," *'eṣah* is a common Biblical word. By a semantic change from counsel, in the sense of advice, the word seems to have taken on the related concept of a council of assembly. In some contexts in the Manual of Discipline the word appears to refer to a group within the community (the *yaḥad*), and in others it appears to be used synonymously with the *yaḥah.* In this latter sense the term may signify "the men of God's counsel," "the party of God," or "the holy party."

Dupont-Sommer has suggested that the use of the term *'eṣah* as a designation of the "party" par-excellence may give us a clue to the etymology of the word Essene. The difficulty of accounting for the word Essene is generally recognized. C. D. Ginsburg said, "There is hardly an expression the etymology of which has called forth such a diversity of opinion as this name has elicited." Of the twenty suggestions which Ginsburg gives, a derivation from the name of the pre-Maccabean party known as the Hasidim has been preferred.

The Greek words used of the Essenes, *essenoi* and *essaioi* have in common the root *ess* which, Dupont-Sommer points out, would be an exact rendering of the Hebrew *'eṣ.* If this suggestion is accepted, Essenes are, literally, "the men of the party" and the identification of the Essenes with the Qumran sect is proved. While much evidence points in that direction it is only fair to note that caution must be exercised in making dogmatic identifications at this stage of our knowledge.

3. The Congregation (*'edah*)

The Qumran community considered itself as united "for a holy congregation" (i.e. — to be a holy congregation). The term is frequently used in the Old Testament. Israel is spoken of as "the congregation of God" (Psalm 82:1); "the congregation of Yahweh" (Numbers 27:17, 31:16; Joshua 22:16-17; Psalm 74:2). The terms "congregation of Israel" and "congregation of the people" are of frequent occurrence. In the Zadokite work the sect is called "the congregation of men dedicated to the perfection of holiness."

The term *'edah* is rendered *sunagoge* in the Septuagint (127 times). It speaks of the "gathering" of the people of God. Since the Qumran community considered itself the true Israel, those terms which had been used of God's people in the Old Testament were appropriated by them and applied exclusively to themselves.

4. Men of the Covenant (*berith*)

The Qumran community, availing itself of the terminology of the Old Testament, applied the term "covenant" to itself. The Zadokite work speaks of "the men who had entered into the New Covenant" when describing those who were faithful to God. The Manual of Discipline describes "a covenant of loyalty" (1:8). While the term New Covenant, or New Testament immediately brings to mind the teachings of the New Testament concerning the work of Christ, it should be remembered that the pre-Christian Qumran community based its terminology on the writings of Jeremiah (31:31-33) who prophesied concerning a "new covenant."

5. Other Names

In addition to the names enumerated there are numerous other ways in which the members of the Qumran community describe themselves. In the Manual of Discipline they are "sons of light" (1:9), "sons of righteousness" (3:20), and "sons of truth" (4:6). The Manual of Discipline does not allow us to consider the Qumran community as religiously self-satisfied however. The members are very conscious of their own failings in spiritual attainment. They see themselves, however, as God's people, "the men of God's lot" (2:2) in contrast with the wicked world without. They are the "volunteers" or "dedicated ones" (5:8) who are "sons of an eternal council" (2:25). As members of the community they are "the perfect of way" (4:22).

B. Names by Which Outsiders Were Identified.

By contrast those who are not members of the community are described as "sons of darkness" (1:10) or "sons of perversion" (3:21). They are "treacherous men" (2:10) and "men of the pit" (9:22). Under "the dominion of Belial" (1:18) they are described as "men of Belial's lot" (2:4-5).

C. Membership in the Qumran Community.

The Manual of Discipline makes it clear that members of the Qumran community had come from among the priests, the

Levites, and the lay members of the Jewish community. The priests who may have separated themselves from the Sadduceean priesthood because of the increasing worldliness of that group, continued to have a place of prominence in the organization, comprising something of a hierarchy. This is, in fact, one of the points of contrast between Qumran and the Christian church which recognized no priestly caste, hereditary or appointed, but considered all believers as possessing a priestly ministry under their great High Priest, Jesus Christ.

When gathering together in the assembly we read that "the priests shall sit down first, then the elders, second; then the rest of all the people shall sit down, each in his own place." (5:2-3). In the gatherings of the community "the priests shall pass over first in order, according to their spirits, one after another; and the Levites shall pass over after them, and all of the people shall pass over third in order . . ." (2:19-21).

It was the duty of the priests to pronounce the blessings on "all the men of God's lot who walk perfectly in all his ways" (2:1-2). The priestly benediction is a paraphrase of Numbers 6:26: "May he bless you with all good and keep you from all evil; may he enlighten your heart with life-giving prudence and be gracious to you with eternal knowledge, may he lift up his loving countenance to you for eternal peace" (2:2-4).

When the community assembled together for the common meal, the priest was called upon to "stretch out his hand first to pronounce a blessing on the first portion of the bread and the wine" (6:5). While much has been made of this meal and its supposed relationship to the Lord's Supper by some writers, there is nothing recorded concerning it in the Qumran scrolls which differs in any marked way from the orthodox Jewish method of beginning a meal with a blessing. The difference is that, instead of the head of the house pronouncing the blessing, the priest is called upon to do so. In one sense it is not wrong to speak of this as a sacrament, if it is remembered that every meal in a Jewish home was so regarded. In blessing the bread and wine at the Last Supper, Jesus was abiding by normal Jewish usage. Orthodox Jews today "break bread" before meals. It was the meaning which Jesus placed upon the breaking of bread and passing of the cup which distinguishes the Last Supper from the ordinary Jewish meal.

In contrast to the blessings pronounced by the priests, the Levites were called upon to pronounce curses upon the wicked: "Accursed may you be for all your wicked, guilty works; may God make you a thing of abhorrence at the hands of all those that wreak vengeance and send after you destruction at the hands of all those that pay recompense; accursed may you be without mercy according to the darkness of your works, and may you suffer wrath in the deep darkness of eternal fire. May God not be gracious to you when you call, and may he not pardon, forgiving your iniquities; may he lift up his angry countenance for vengeance upon you, and may there be no peace for you at the mouth of all those that hold enmity" (1:21–2:5).

We are reminded of the words of Jesus in Matthew 5:43, "Ye have heard that it hath been said, 'Thou shalt love thy neighbour and hate thine enemy.'" Jesus spoke scathing words to the self-righteous hypocrite, but New Testament ethics and attitudes were markedly different from the attitudes expressed in the Levites' curses.

In addition to the priests and Levites it is estimated that there were several hundred lay members of the Qumran community. Men, women, and children are included, as is clearly indicated in line four of the appendix to the Manual of Discipline. The remains of women are also found in the cemetery near Khirbet Qumran. Since Josephus spoke of a group of marrying Essenes, the presence of women at Qumran does not pose a problem in the identification of the Qumran community as Essene.

The term volunteers (*mitnabbim*) describes the members of the Qumran community. They were convinced that the Graeco-Roman society of their day was corrupt and that the Jews who had made their peace with that society were apostate. They were going out into the wilderness to "prepare the way of the Lord" (8:14). This was to be accomplished by rigorous discipline willingly assumed by each member of the community.

D. Initiation into the Qumran Community.

While all who were born into Jewish homes considered themselves Jews, to become a member of the Qumran community, the "true Israel," was a difficult undertaking. The volunteer must first present himself to the overseer of the group for a kind of preliminary examination. If the overseer was satisfied that he might be a fit member of the community he was admitted "into the covenant to turn to the truth and to turn away from all wickedness" (6:14-15).

After a probationary period of undisclosed length, the candidate appears before "the council of the many" (i.e. the formal congregation of the community) and is examined "concerning his affairs, and as the lot falls out, according to the council of the many, he draws near or departs" (6:16). If he passes this examination, he is placed on probation for a year. During this time he is considered a member of the community, but he does not partake of the common meals of the community nor share its wealth. Presumably he does not turn his own wealth over to the community during this probationary period.

A further examination takes place at the close of this first year. If "the many" are satisfied with his progress "they shall bring his wealth and property to the man who is the Supervisor of the property of the many, and they shall be recorded to his account at his disposal (lit. at his hand), but not for the many shall he spend it (lit. bring it forth)" (6:19-20). The property of the man is separately recorded so that it may be returned to him should he leave the community before becoming a full member. Even after showing satisfactory progress after his year's probation "he shall not touch the drink of the many until he has completed a second year among the men of the community" (6:20-21).

A final examination takes place at the close of the second year of probation. If successful, the candidate is enrolled "in the order of his assigned position in the midst of his brethren . . ." (6:22). He is now a full-fledged member subject to all the privileges and responsibilities of the community.

Each year the community solemnly gathers to review the progress made during the previous year. Priests, then Levites, and finally laymen solemnly march in battle formation, each individual in the position which he has merited: "They shall be registered in order, one after the other, according to his understanding and performance, so that every one of them shall obey his neighbor, the lesser obeying the greater; and so that they shall have an investigation of their spirit and their performance year by year, so as to promote each one according to his understanding and the perfection of his way, or put him back according to his perversions . . ." (5:23-24).

Josephus in his *Wars of the Jews* speaks of the strict discipline of the Essenes. The individual member of the community was obliged to live in constant subjection to his overseer: ". . . they do nothing but according to the injunctions of their curators; only these two things are done among them at every one's own free will, which are, to assist those that want it, and to shew mercy; for they are permitted of their own accord to afford succor to such as deserve it, when they stand in need of it, and to bestow food on those that are in distress, but they cannot give anything to their kindred without the curators" (ii, 8:6).

E. Life in the Qumran Community.

1. Water Purification

Unlike Christian baptism, the ceremonial lustrations of the Qumran community were not an initiatory rite. They were a part of the daily life of the full-fledged member of the community.

Josephus, in describing the daily life of the Essenes, tells us that at the fifth hour of the day "they assemble themselves together . . . into one place, and when they have clothed themselves in white veils, they then bathe their bodies in cold water" (*op. cit.* ii, 8:5). The archaeological remains of Khirbet Qumran indicate the provision made for "purification" by the builders of the community center.

The Manual of Discipline alludes to the fact that ceremonial lustrations are a part of the life of the community, but warns against the assumption that cleansing in water is meritorious in itself. "He (the sinner) shall not be absolved by expiations, nor purified by waters of ablution nor sanctified by sea and rivers, nor purified by all the waters that wash. Unclean, unclean he shall be as long as he despises the commandments of God, not being instructed in the communion of his counsel. But in a spirit of true counsel in regard to the ways of a man, all his iniquities will be atoned so that he may contemplate the light of life" (3:4-8).

The New Testament makes it clear that ceremonial washings were characteristic of first century Judaism. It was not in the area of personal hygiene, but of ceremonial cleansings that Jesus said, ". . . to eat with unwashen hands defileth not a man" (Matthew 15:20). The Qumran water purifications have more in common with the "washing of hands" in Matthew 15 than they do with Christian baptism.

2. The Common Meal

As with water purifications, so in the case of the common meal, only full members of the community could participate. In the same context in which Josephus described the lustrations of the Essenes he says, ". . . they go, after a pure manner, into the dining-room, as into a certain holy temple, and quietly set themselves down: upon which the baker lays them loaves in order; the cook also brings a single plate of one sort of food, and sets it before every one of them; but a priest says grace before meat, and it is unlawful for any one to taste of the food before grace be said. The same priest, when he hath dined, says grace again after meat, and when they begin and when they end they praise God as he that bestows their food upon them, after which they lay aside their (white) garments and betake themselves to their labors until the evening. Then they return home to supper after the same manner . . . (*op. cit.* ii, 8:5).

The Manual of Discipline emphasizes the fact that the community partakes of its meals as a unit. "Together they shall eat, together they shall bless, together they shall take counsel" (6:2-3). The meal was begun with the priest's blessing. It should be emphasized that the meal was a "sacred meal" or, as some term it, "a sacrament" in the sense that every meal to a pious Jew is a sacrament. An objection to this statement may be made in view of the fact that novices who had not completed two years of probation were not permitted to partake of the common meal. The meal, however, was expressive of the unity of the community, and the novices were not yet members of the community. Jesus did not adopt an Essene rite. He did adapt a Jewish custom of "breaking bread" and "blessing" God for His bounty, using the broken bread and the cup as symbols of his body and blood.

3. The Study of Scripture

Following the passage in the Manual of Discipline which describes the common meals of the group we read of the provision made for the reading, study, and expounding of the law: "And in whatever place there be ten men, there shall not cease to be a man who studies the law day and night, constantly, concerning the duties of one toward the other. And let 'the many' keep awake together a third of all the nights of the year in order to read the Book, to study the law, and to worship together" (6:6-8).

The group of ten is the quorum (Hebrew: *minyan*) necessary for the conduct of a service of worship, still observed in orthodox synagogues. In these groups a "round-the-clock" vigil was kept. Members of the community had to spend a portion of their nights in the study of the law, and prayer. This was in addition to their hard manual labor and the devotions of each day. It may be presumed that the members were divided into three groups who took turns in reading the law, commenting on it, and offering their praise to God. Evidently during the day certain of the community were relieved of their usual responsibilities in order that the chain of Bible study and devotion might not be broken.

We learn of the regard of the Qumran community for the Bible from other Qumran manuscripts, also. Copies of the books of the Bible, commentaries on the sacred books, allusions and quotations from the Bible in the sectarian documents, particularly the Thanksgiving Psalms bear testimony to the fact that the Qumran Community owed its very life to the Scriptures.

F. Government of the Qumran Community.

The government of the Qumran community had democratic elements with a supreme court or council in which final authority was vested. This is summarized in the Manual of Discipline: "It is according to the decision of the Sons of Zadok, the priests who keep the Covenant, and according to the decision of the majority of the members of the community, those who hold firmly to the covenant and according to their judgment that the decision of the lot shall pronounce in everything relating to the law or property, or judgment" (9:7).

A priest had the duty of presiding over each unit of ten members: "In every place where there shall be ten men of the council of the community there shall not be absent from them a priest. Each according to his position they shall sit before him; and thus they shall be asked for their counsel regarding everything" (6:3-4). The priests held special responsibilities for "only the sons of Aaron shall administer judgment and wealth, and according to their judgment the lot shall determine with regard to every regulation concerning the members of the community" (9:7).

Final authority was vested in the council of twelve (or fifteen) men: "There shall be in the council of the community twelve men, and there shall be three priests who are perfect in all that has been revealed of the whole law . . ." (8:1-2). It is probable that the council consisted of twelve individuals, three of whom were priests. While the priests had positions of honor and responsibility it should be noted that the laity was numerically stronger than the priestly element in the council.

Other leaders are mentioned as having specifically defined responsibilities. "The supervisor (*mebaqqer*) of the property of the many" (6:20) was the custodian of the material goods and bookkeeper for the community. The overseer, or inspector (*paqid*) of the group examined the candidates and determined whether or not to admit them to the community as probationers. We are not told how these officers were chosen, nor whether or not they had to be priests. It may be presumed that they were elected officers.

G. Property in the Qumran Community.

The fully-initiated member of the Qumran community intended to dedicate everything he possessed to the movement: "And all who have offered themselves for His truth shall bring all their mind, and strength and wealth into the community of God, to purify their minds by the truth of God's statutes, and to control their strength according to the perfection of His ways and all their wealth according to His righteous counsel" (1:11-13). It is not until the period of probation was ended that the property of the individual was added to "the goods of the community" (7:6-7).

Philo of Alexandria, in *Quod Omnis Probus Liber* (c. A.D. 20) wrote of the Essenes, "They had a storehouse, common expenditure, common raiments, common food eaten in Syssitia or common meals. This was made possible by their practice of putting whatever they each earned day by day into a common fund, out of which also the sick were supported when they could not work" (paragraphs 85-86).

An interesting rule relates to the possible harm done to the property of the community: "If (one) commits a fraud against the wealth of the community, causing its loss, he shall repay it in full. If he is not able to pay it he shall be punished sixty days" (7:6-8). We wonder how an individual who had turned over his possessions to the community could find the means of paying for such damage. It is possible that this provision applied to novices rather than full members of the community.

H. Rules of the Qumran Community.

The fact that the Qumran Community was subject to rigorous discipline has been previously noted. Examples of specific rules may evoke a smile from a twentieth-century reader, but they were serious business to the members of the ancient community.

The assemblies of the "many" must be accorded due reverence. If an individual lies down and goes to sleep during one of the sessions he is to be punished for a period of thirty days (7:10). Perhaps one of the members who had spent the night in reading and expounding Scripture would be tempted to catch a few winks during the "business meetings." Spitting in the midst of a session of "the many" brings a thirty day sentence also (7:13). Should one of the members be tempted to leave a session of "the many" he runs the risk of discipline, for "the man who departs from a session of the many without permission and without good reason, up to three times during one session, shall be punished ten days" (7:10-11). Parliamentary procedure is observed, for the rules say, "A man shall not speak in the midst of his neighbor's words, before his brother finishes speaking" (6:10). The penalty for infraction of this rule is ten days of punishment (7:9).

Slander is a serious matter. "A man who slanders his neighbor shall be separated for a year from the sacred food of the many, and he shall be punished; and a man who slanders the many is to be dismissed from among them and shall not come back again" (7:16-17).

Even in the Qumran community there were temptations to apostasy. "If a man's spirit wavers from the institution of the community, so that he becomes a traitor to the truth and walks in the stubbornness of his heart; if he repents he shall be punished two years" (7:18-19).

The temptation to keep a portion of the property was evidently too much for some members of the community. One of the laws says, "If there is found among them a man who consciously lies about his wealth, he shall be excluded from the sacred food of the many for a year, and shall be deprived of a fourth of his food ration" (6:25). We are reminded of the sin of Ananias and Sapphira as recorded in Acts 5.

I. The Theology of the Qumran Community.

1. Messiah

Our word "Messiah" is a transliteration of a Hebrew word meaning "anointed." Its Greek equivalent gives us our word "Christ." In Old Testament usage the king was frequently spoken of as "the Lord's anointed." Similarly the sons of Aaron were "anointed" for their priestly ministry. The term "messiah" (with a small "m"; there is no distinction in Hebrew) can apply to any king or priest according to Old Testament usage. Even Cyrus, the Persian king, is so designated (Isaiah 45:1).

In the prophetic portions of the Old Testament the attention of Israel was focused upon a coming age in which the enemies of God would be confounded, and the earth would be "filled with the knowledge of the glory of the Lord as the waters cover the sea" (cf. Habakkuk 2:14). In this coming age an "anointed one" or "Messiah" would rule in righteousness (Isaiah 32:1).

When we meet the term "Messiah" in the scrolls it is necessary for us to determine from the context whether we are dealing with an ordinary priest or king, or with the prophesied future Messiah.

A passage in the Manual of Discipline which seems clearly to point to a future Messiah states, "They shall not depart from any counsel of the law, walking in all the stubbornness of their hearts; but they shall judge by the first judgments by which the men of the community began to be disciplined, until there shall come a prophet and the Messiahs of Aaron and Israel" (9:9-11).

Early rabbinic writings contain a doctrine of two Messiahs: the king (descended from David) and the priest (descended from Aaron) of the future. The passage quoted seems to state that the members of the community are to live lives of obedience to the laws which were given to them, "the first judgments" or "first laws," until a future Messiah (or Messiahs) should arise in the last days to give a final revelation. The reference to a coming prophet is an echo of Deuteronomy 18:18.

If the concept of an "anointed one" or "anointed ones" at Qumran seems confused, it should be remembered that the New Testament writers see in Jesus the fulfillment of prophetic priestly, and kingly functions, all of which are clearly taught as subject to Messianic fulfillment in the Old Testament. The Davidic genealogy of Jesus would seem to bar him from the priestly office, but the author of Hebrews seeks to show that Jesus is a priest, not after the order of Levi, but from a better and older order – that of Melchizedek. That those who pondered the Scriptures of the Old Testament before the advent of Christ should have been perplexed, and that those perplexities sometimes resulted in very strange teachings can be readily understood. Qumran Messianism is discussed in greater detail in Chapter 11.

2. The Law

As a corollary to the study of Scripture, which was basic in Qumran thought and practice, we might expect an attitude toward Old Testament regulations similar to that of the Pharisees described in the New Testament. Such is not the case.

Candidates for admission to the community were examined "with regard to . . . understanding and . . . performance of the law" (5:21). In being received into the community the member "shall take it upon himself by a binding oath to turn to the law of Moses, according to all that he commanded, with all his heart and with all his soul, to all that is revealed of it to the sons of Zadok, the priests who keep the covenant and seek His will" (5:8-9).

There are evidences, however, that the interpretation of the law at Qumran differed in some instances from the interpretations of Pharisaic Judaism. The statement that the community should walk in the "first judgments" (9:9) seems to be a protest against innovations. Perhaps the "oral traditions" which Jesus criticized were also known and rejected at Qumran, as they were by the medieval Karaites. Although practicing ceremonial lustrations we know that the Qumran community emphasized the inner, spiritual requirements for forgiveness, "for they will not be cleansed unless they have turned from their evil" (5:13-14).

The absence of any mention of animal sacrifice in the Manual of Discipline has been noted. The Qumran community considered that its spiritual principles would constitute "a ransom for the guilt of transgression and sinful faithlessness." "Atonement will be made for the land more effectively than by the flesh of whole burnt offerings and the fat of sacrifices. The offering of the lips will be in justice like the pleasing quality of righteousness, and perfect conduct like a free-will gift of an acceptable offering" (9:3-5).

Discussing the Essenes, Josephus says, ". . . they do not offer sacrifices, because they have more pure lustrations of their own" (*Antiquities of the Jews*, xviii, i, 5). Philo, however, says that they "did not sacrifice animals, regarding a reverent mind as the only true sacrifice" (*Quod Omnis Probus Liber*).

The Zadokite document, on the other hand, indicates that the sect which produced it still considered Jerusalem as its sanctuary and took part in the sacrifices offered there (13:27). If the Zadokites were a group of priests who separated from the materialistically-minded Jerusalem priesthood, as we have reason to assume, their progress of thought seems to have developed along the lines of increasing independence. First insisting on the validity of sacrifices in the Jerusalem Temple only as they accorded with their own regulations (*Zadokite Fragments* 8:12-20), they seem to have advanced to the place where they denied the value of the sacrifices entirely. Deeming the priesthood apostate, they refused to recognize the validity of the Jerusalem sacrifices.

This is, of course, one of the many places where contrasts can be drawn between Jesus and his followers and the Essenes. Although critical of those who had made His Father's house "a den of thieves" (Luke 19:46), and severely criticizing the Pharisees, Sadducees, and scribes, Jesus went to Jerusalem at the time of the observances of sacred days in the Jewish calendar, was crucified at the time of the Passover, and sent His Spirit when Jews from all parts of the ancient world were in Jerusalem to celebrate the feast of Pentecost. It will be remembered that in Acts 3 we read of Peter and John in the Temple at Jerusalem at the hour of prayer.

3. Election

The Qumran community strongly believed in the doctrine of divine election. In describing the differences in theology among the Jewish "sects," Josephus mentions this as a characteristic of Essenes: "At this time there were three sects among the Jews, who had different opinions concerning human actions; the one was called the sect of the Pharisees, another the sect of the Sadducees, and another the sect of the Essenes. Now for the Pharisees, they say that some actions, but not all, are the work of fate, and some of them are in our own power, and that they are liable to fate, but are not caused by fate. But the sect of the Essenes affirm, that fate governs all things, and that nothing befalls men but what is according to its determination. And for the Sadducees, they take away fate, and say there is no such thing, and that the events of human affairs are not at its disposal; but they suppose that all our actions are in our own power, so that we are ourselves the causes of what is good, and receive what is evil from our own folly," *Antiquities of the Jews*, xiii, 5:9. It may be observed that the more secularly minded group (the Sadducees) placed exclusive emphasis on human freedom, and the most other-worldly group (the Essenes) placed exclusive emphasis on the Divine sovereignty. In using the term "fate," Josephus was seeking to use language which would be understood by his Gentile readers.

An oft-recurring word (14 times) in the Manual of Discipline is the Hebrew word which is translated "lot" (*goral*). It is used in two related senses. In certain contexts it speaks of man's "lot" in life, the destiny allotted by God to each individual. In others it speaks of the two divisions of mankind. The righteous are "the men of the lot of God," and the wicked are "the men of the lot of Belial."

A clear statement of sovereignty is noted in the following: "from the God of knowledge comes all that is and ever was. Before they came into being, He established the design of them. And after they came into being, according to their design, they perform their task; and nothing can be changed" (3:15-17).

Election is clearly taught: "To those whom God has chosen, he has given them for an eternal possession; he has given them an inheritance in the lot of the holy ones and has joined them in communion with the sons of heaven to form one congregation, a company of a holy building for an eternal planting" (11:7-8).

The confidence and security of the member of the Qumran community is also noted: "Blessed art thou, O my God, who openest the heart of thy servant to knowledge. Direct all his works in righteousness and establish the son of thy handmaid, as thou didst accept the elect of mankind to stand before thee forever. For without thee conduct will not be blameless, and apart from thy will nothing will be done. It is thou that hast taught all knowledge; and everything that has come to pass has been by thy will" (11:15-18).

Yet this assurance of possession of the true revelation of God, and thus of being the true people of God, was accompanied by an acute sense of sinfulness. Man "was kneaded of dust, and the food of worms is his portion. He is an emission of spittle, a cut-off bit of clay, and his desire is for the dust" (11:21). It is only "of the Lord's mercies that we are not consumed" (Lamentations 3:22). Being weak, and utterly dependent upon God there was no room for pride.

4. Responsibility

Neither at Qumran nor in Christian theology has an emphasis on divine sovereignty and election served as a denial of the doctrine of human responsibility. The member of the community vows "to be separated from all the men of error who walk in the way of wickedness. For these are not reckoned in His covenant, for they have not sought or searched for Him in His statutes, to know the hidden things in which they have gone astray, incurring guilt, and with reference to the things revealed they have acted with a high hand, arousing anger leading to judgment . . ." (5:11-12).

Before a holy God the member of the Qumran community was aware of the fact that it was only of God's sovereign grace that he was among the chosen. Yet, as he contemplated the wicked, he knew that their sinfulness was the occasion of God's displeasure.

We meet the same theology and same morality in the Old Testament. When Joseph, in Egypt, said to his brothers, "It was not you who sent me here, but God," he was expressing more than a spirit of forgiveness. From one point of view the brothers had sinned and had to suffer for their evil doing. From another point of view, God had sent Joseph into Egypt "to preserve life" (Genesis 45:4, 8). While incomprehensible to the mind of man, human responsibility and divine sovereignty are complementary, not contradictory doctrines in the Old Testament, Qumran, and the New Testament.

5. The Calendar

To the members of the Qumran community, complete obedience to the law of God included the necessity of observing sacred days in accord with a correct calendar. They vowed "not to transgress in any one of all the words of God in their appointed times; not to advance their times or postpone any of the appointed seasons; not to turn aside from the ordinances of God's truth, going to the right or to the left" (1:13-15). Peoples using different calendars observe their festivals on different days. The date of Christmas was a source of contention between theologians of the Eastern Church and Western Christendom. Sabbatarians are opposed to modern movements for calendar reform because of the necessity for using a calendar that divides time in accordance with the needs of the religious calendar.

The Book of Jubilees, one of the books in the collection of ancient Jewish writings to which the term pseudepigrapha is applied by Protestant writers (Catholics call them "apocrypha"), describes a calendar of 364 days, divided into four seasons of three months each, thirteen weeks to a season. Each month had thirty days, with one day intercalated for each of the four seasons. There were exactly fifty-two weeks in the year. Thus the festivals would recur on exactly the same day.

The Book of Enoch states that the angel Uriel revealed this calendar to Enoch, who passed it on to Methusaleh.

Barthelemy argues that this was the calendar in general use at the beginning of the Hellenistic period, and Julian Morgenstern thinks that it was originally of Amorite or Canaanite origin. It was used by the medieval Karaites. Rabbinical, "normative" Judaism, however, used a lunar calendar divided into thirteen months of twenty-eight days, with an intercalating month added three times in eight years. This was the calendar used in Babylon.

Copies of both the Book of Jubilees and the Book of Enoch have been found at Qumran. Some have suggested that the Qumran community, or their spiritual forebearers, the Hasidim, produced these works. In any event, the use of the proper calendar became one of the marks of orthodoxy to the Qumran community.

6. Dualism

A large section of the Manual of Discipline (3:13–4:26) and the entire "War Scroll" discuss the contrast between good and evil, light and darkness. This terminology is familiar from the New Testament and will be discussed more fully when we consider the War Scroll. It may be noted here, however, that it is an over-simplification to trace the concept of a battle between the forces of light (righteousness) and the forces of darkness (sin) to Iranian influences. That the Iranians faced the problem of the existence of evil in the world and developed a dualism wherein the forces of good and evil were nearly equalized is true. It is equally true that the Sumerians and Babylonians of remote Near Eastern history discussed battles among their gods reflecting the same struggle. Thinking man in every cultural environment faces the problem of evil.

The Biblical doctrine of Satan treats the same problems, but on a different basis. If the ancient inhabitants of Mesopotamia (along with many other peoples) fancied a pantheon of good and evil deities, and if the Iranians reduced them to two, the Bible speaks of but one God by whom all else was created. According to Biblical theology, Satan is a rebellious creature of God, whom God in his inscrutable wisdom permits to exercise limited freedom and power (cf. Job 1) until the purposes of God for this world are consummated. This concept both protects the Oneness of God and accounts for the presence of evil in the world.

While it is not our responsibility to prove the orthodoxy of the Qumran community – and in some areas we must underscore their heterodoxy, it is gratifying to note the way in which their description of the two spirits in man agrees with the Biblical representation. "All that is and ever was comes from the God of knowledge" (3:15) is a clear statement of God's Oneness. Evil is discussed but, it is evil in a world which is ultimately subject to its Creator. "He created man to have dominion over the world and appointed for him two spirits, that he might walk by them until the appointed time of his visitation; they are the spirits of truth and of error" (3:17-18). Identifying the spirits, we read, "In the hand of the Prince of Lights is dominion over all sons of righteousness; in the ways of light they walk. And in the hand of the angel of darkness is all dominion over the sons of error; and in the ways of darkness they walk. And through the angel of darkness is the straying of all the sons of righteousness, and all their sin and their iniquities and their guilt, and the transgressions of their works are the result of his dominion, according to the mysteries of God, until the time, appointed by Him. All their afflictions and the appointed times of their distress are due to the dominion of his enmity. And all the spirits of his lot try to make the sons of light stumble; but the God of Israel and the angel of His truth have helped all the sons of light . . ." (3:20-25).

The Qumran community conceived of a battle in progress within the individual soul somewhat analagous to that described by Paul in Galatians 5:17: "For the flesh lusteth against the Spirit, and the Spirit against the flesh: and these are contrary the one to the other . . ." All men are under the mastery of one or the other of the two spirits which vie for the mastery over men until the "appointed time of visitation" when God will destroy evil and "make the upright perceive the knowledge of the Most High and the wisdom of the sons of heaven."

As Millar Burrows points out, the dualism discussed here is one of good and evil, not of spirit and matter. For this reason he rejects the thought that the Qumran community was subject to Gnostic influences.

II. The Habakkuk Commentary

The Habakkuk Commentary from Cave 1, Qumran, consists of thirteen columns of text written on a scroll made of two strips of soft leather sewed end to end with linen thread. The writing was done on the hair side which was carefully dressed and is smooth to the touch. The beginning of the scroll, apparently one column, is lost. At the bottom of each column a few lines of text are missing. The right hand margin of column one has disintegrated and is lost. The scroll, of course, reads from right to left. The middle of column two is also missing. In its present form the scroll measures five feet in length and is five and one-half inches at its maximum height. It was published with the

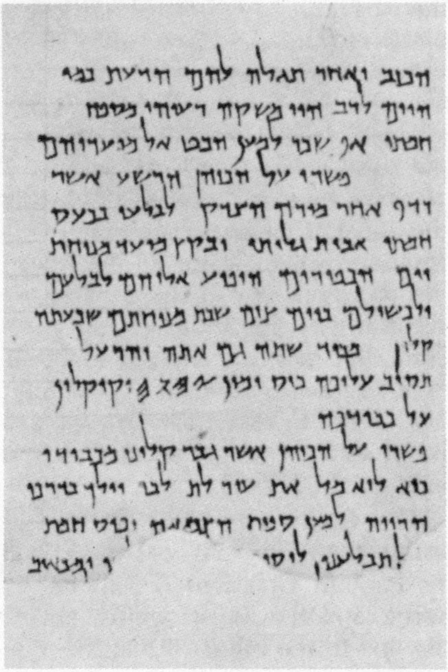

A COLUMN FROM THE HABBAKUK COMMENTARY from Cave 1. Courtesy, American Schools of Oriental Research.

St. Mark's Isaiah Scroll [1QIsa[a]] by the American Schools of Oriental Research in 1950.

From the standpoint of Biblical interpretation the Habakkuk Commentary has no value. It will not throw light on any Biblical passage. From the standpoint of the history of the Qumran community and the use made of canonical Scripture by sectarian Judaism it is of great value.

The term "midrash" is used of ancient Jewish commentaries which explain Scripture by means of anecdote and legend. The Habakkuk Commentary is not a midrash, but it employs midrashic principles of exegesis. The ancient commentator quotes a portion of Habakkuk, then uses a Hebrew word meaning "its interpretation," after which he relates the writings of Habakkuk (who prophesied in the sixth century before Christ) to the political and religious circumstances of the time of the writing of the commentary (probably the first century before Christ). The Hebrew word for interpretation, *pesher*, gives us the technical name by which scholars now speak of this type of commentary. In symbols the Habakkuk Commentary is 1QpHab – Cave 1, Qumran, *pesher* Habakkuk.

The commentary treats only the first two chapters of the Book of Habakkuk, excluding the psalm which comprises chapter three of the canonical book. It is the prophetic portion of Habakkuk's writings that suited the purposes of the commentator.

The handwriting of the Habakkuk Commentary is the most clear of any that has been published to date. In several places the tetragrammaton (the "four letters" which comprise the consonants in the Hebrew name for God, usually pronounced by scholars Yahweh but not traditionally pronounced at all by Jews who fear breaking the second commandment) is written in early Hebrew script, instead of the square letters which were used in the period of the scrolls, as they are today.

Of importance both in the discussion of the date of the scrolls and the history of the Qumran community are the historical allusions with which the Habakkuk Commentary abounds. With one possible exception, no names of persons known to history occur. To members of the community the references were obvious, to outsiders, they may have been deliberately disguised – perhaps to avoid persecution. The result, as far as we are concerned, is a field day wherein scholars have been able to put forth every conceivable hypothesis. When the scrolls now being pieced together in the Palestine Museum are published, many of our questions may be answered.

A. The Enemy of Israel in the Habakkuk Commentary – The Kittim.

In commenting on Habakkuk 1:6, "For lo, I am rousing the Chaldeans, that bitter and hasty nation" the commentator says, "This means the Kittim, who are swift and mighty in battle, overthrowing rulers and subduing them in the dominion of the Kittim . . ."

The Kittim are clearly foreign invaders or conquerors. The term Kittim occurs in the Hebrew Bible. In the table of nations (Genesis 10) the Kittim appear among the sons of Javan (the Ionians; Greeks). In other passages the Kittim are clearly the inhabitants of the island of Cyprus (Isaiah 23:1, 12; Jeremiah 2:10; Ezekiel 27:6). In Daniel 11:30, in a context referring to the Romans we read, "For ships of Kittim shall come against him," viz. Antiochus Epiphanes. The Septuagint actually reads "ships of the Romans." In the apocryphal I Maccabees, Alexander the Great is said to have come from the land of the Kittim (1:1). The Book of Jubilees also speaks of the Macedonians as Kittim (24:28 f.).

External evidence is not decisive in identifying the Kittim. Cypriots, Greeks (Macedonians), or Romans are so designated. We are thrown back on the internal evidence of the Habakkuk

Commentary and related documents if we hope to make an exact identification. That they are a powerful people we know. Some of the descriptions given in the commentary could apply to any group of invaders. They are "swift and mighty in battle." They "do not believe in the statutes" of the God of Israel. They plan evil, and carry out their plans "with cunning and deceit." They "mock at great ones and despise honored men; of kings and princes they make sport." In their ruthless advance they "cause many to perish by the sword – youths, men, and old men; women and little children – and on the fruit of the womb they have no mercy."

The fact that the Kittim "trample the earth with their horses and with their animals" has been taken as evidence that the Kittim are Macedonians. Adherents of this view interpret "animals" as the war elephants used by the Seleucid kings and pictured by them on some of their coins. It seems more natural, however, to take the word "animals" as a reference to the beasts of burden which accompany an army. If the writer meant to identify the beasts as elephants he could have used the appropriate Hebrew word.

The enigmatic line, "they sacrifice to their standards, and their weapons of war are the object of their worship," has led many scholars to identify the Kittim of the Habakkuk Commentary with the Romans. Secular history tells us of the veneration which the Roman armies paid to their military standards. Josephus states that the Romans who stormed the Jerusalem Temple (A.D. 70) offered sacrifices to their standards at the eastern gate of the Temple. On the other hand it has been argued that Antiochus Epiphanes claimed to be the incarnation of Zeus, and that the banners of his armies may have borne the likeness of the king as Zeus.

While admitting that the evidence for application of the term Kittim to any one nation is inconclusive, Millar Burrows concludes that the cult of standards, other things being equal, favors identification with the Romans. Both the Habakkuk Commentary and the War Scroll appear to have been written in the early days of the Roman occupation of Judea (63 B.C.). This fact favors an identification of the Kittim with the Romans.

B. Important Personages in the Habakkuk Commentary.

1. The Teacher of Righteousness

Of the individuals discussed in the Habakkuk Commentary, the most intriguing is the one named the Teacher of Righteousness, or the Righteous Teacher as the term may otherwise be translated. The term, while not a scriptural one, probably is based on the analogy of the term Teacher of Falsehood (cf. Isaiah 9:14-15; Habakkuk 2:18). It also occurs in the *Zadokite Work*.

The Teacher of Righteousness is considered by some scholars to be the founder of the Qumran community. Whether or not this can be proved, it is certainly true that he became its honored leader. Never identified by name, it is clear from the comment on Habakkuk 1:5 that he was a priest. He was the recipient and means of divine revelation, for "God made him to know all the mysteries of the words of His servants the prophets," and "God placed him in the house of Judah to explain all the words of His servants, the prophets" (Commentary on 2:2 and 1:5). The Teacher of Righteousness did not come with an authoritative "I say unto you" but rather, with a "key to the Scripture" after the pattern of religious sects such as Christian Science. It should be stressed that the Teacher of Righteousness was an interpreter of former revelation, not an independent prophet in his own right.

Although a positive identification of the Teacher of Righteousness may be difficult, if not impossible, certain of his characteristics are clear. His life was that of a strict ascetic. Learned teacher that he was, he was able to attract a considerable following. His interpretations of the prophets and, presumably, the law, were considered binding on his followers. Habakkuk 2:4, "The just shall live by his faith" is interpreted by the words: "This means all the doers of the law in the house of Judah, whom God will rescue from the house of judgment because of their labor and their faith in the Teacher of Righteousness." This is not faith in an act of atonement, similar to Christian faith, but faith in a great teacher of the law.

Commenting on Habakkuk 1:13, the Habakkuk Commentary says, ". . . into the hand of his elect God will deliver the judgment of all the nations. . . ." Dupont-Sommer maintains that the expression "his elect" refers to the Teacher of Righteousness who is God's agent in the judgment of the nations and Israel in the eyes of the commentator. As Burrows points out, however, "elect" is probably to be considered as plural in meaning (although grammatically singular), referring to the "elect of God" or the people who are the followers of the Teacher of Righteousness. Thus the whole passage states that the (heathen, unbelieving) nations will not destroy God's people, but rather God's people, his elect, will be the means by which God destroys the wicked.

2. The Wicked Priest

Opposed to the Teacher of Righteousness is "the man of the lie," otherwise called "the Wicked Priest" or "the priest who rebelled." The person of whom Habakkuk says, "Woe to him who heaps up, and it is not his own" (2:6) is said by the commentator to be "the wicked priest who enjoyed a reputation for truth when he first took office; but when he had begun to rule in Israel, his heart was lifted up and he forsook God and betrayed His statutes for the sake of wealth. He plundered and assembled the wealth like men of violence who rebel against God. He took the wealth of peoples, adding to himself the penalty of guilt. He practiced abomination in all impurity and filth."

This does not give us any definite clue concerning the identity of the Wicked Priest, for the description could well apply to many historical personages. Evidently he began well, subsequently became proud, forsook God and the law, amassed wealth by violent means and became famous (at least among his enemies) for his wickedness.

Dupont-Sommer who thinks of the Teacher of Righteousness as an anticipation of Christ makes a restoration of the missing last line in column 8 (dealing with Habakkuk 2:8) in which he reads that the Teacher of Righteousness was "smitten by him" (i.e. the Wicked Priest) by virtue of "wicked judgements" (i.e. the Wicked Priest's judgments). We cannot assert that such a restoration is impossible, nor should we be alarmed if it were proved true. The history of religion is dotted with martyrdoms, and this would be but another in the series. It seems more likely, however, that the description is of God's judgment on the wickedness of the Wicked Priest. The priest who had proudly rejected God and His law was humiliated by the judgment of God which fell upon him.

C. The Problem of Identification.

The identification in history of the Teacher of Righteousness, and his counterpart, the Wicked Priest, has been the subject of much scholarly debate. Plausible theories have been offered, but positive identification is still not possible. The principal viewpoints cluster around the events of the period immediately preceding the Maccabean revolt and the events which preceded the taking of Jerusalem by Pompey's armies. It will be noted that the identification of the Kittim with Greeks or Romans has important bearing on the identification of the Teacher of Righteousness and the Wicked Priest.

1. Pre-Maccabean

Josephus and the second book of Maccabees tell of the high priest Onias III who was an example of godliness. A victim of politics and intrigue, he was supplanted by his brother Jason, then murdered by his brother's successor, Menelaus. Onias died in 171 B.C. Of Menelaus it is said, "He came to Jerusalem bringing nothing worthy of the high priesthood, but having the passion of a cruel tyrant and the rage of a savage beast."

Jason and Menelaus cooperated with the Seleucid rulers of Syria in their attempt to force Greek customs and religion upon the Jews. In 168 or 167 B.C. Menelaus, in collaboration with Antiochus Epiphanes, desecrated the Temple. The comments on Habakkuk 2:17 in the Habakkuk Commentary assert, "this means the city, that is Jerusalem, in which the wicked priest wrought abominable works and defiled God's sanctuary."

In the appointment of Jason in the place of Onias III the orthodox in Israel were shocked that the sacred office could be sold to the highest bidder. When Jason was set aside in favor of Menelaus, however, the orthodox were enraged for, not only was the sacred office commercialized, but the Zadokite line, reaching back to Solomon's priest, was set aside. The emphasis in the Habakkuk Commentary on "the sons of Zadok" is thought to be an indication that the origin of the sect is related to the removal of Onias III.

As a result of the period of persecution associated with Antiochus Epiphanes "many seekers for uprightness and justice went down into the wilderness to settle, with their sons and their wives and their cattle, because their hardships had become so severe" (I Maccabees 2:29-30). The Manual of Discipline says of the Qumran community that they shall be "separated from the midst of the session of the men of error to go to the wilderness to prepare there the way of HW'H' (i.e. Yahweh)" (8:13). Thus one school of thought concludes that the Teacher of Righteousness and the Wicked Priest are personages who lived in the Maccabean period. H. H. Rowley defended the view that Onias III was the Teacher of Righteousness and Menelaus was the Wicked Priest.

2. John Hyrcanus

It will be recalled that during the reign of John Hyrcanus (134-104 B.C.) a rupture with the party of the Pharisees was occasioned by the demand on the part of an individual named Eleazar, or Judah, that Hyrcanus "lay down the High-priesthood." It has been conjectured that this extremist among the Pharisees may have become an Essene leader.

The description of an Essene named Judah (or Judas, in its Greek form) in the writings of Josephus has suggested parallels with the descriptions of the Teacher of Righteousness in the scrolls. Both were teachers who had attracted a group of loyal disciples. Judah taught about predictive prophecy and the Teacher of Righteousness was deemed a teacher of prophecy whose views were binding on his followers. Judah the Essene was hostile toward the official Jerusalem priesthood, as was the Teacher of Righteousness. The Wicked Priest who attacked the Teacher of Righteousness probably did so in the Temple area.

By combining the descriptions of Judah, the Pharisee who defied John Hyrcanus, and Judah the Essene, described by Josephus, a case has been made for this Judah as the founder of the Essenes and the Teacher of Righteousness.

3. Aristobulus I

In the comments on Habakkuk 2:7-8, which refer to torments and tortures, we read of the Wicked Priest with "horrors of sore diseases" and "vengeance in his body of flesh." John Hyrcanus died in peace, but his successor, Aristobulus I died in terrible agony after a rule of about a year. An argument has been made for more than one Wicked Priest: the concept of the false priesthood against the true priesthood. In this view, Aristobulus I would be one of a series of "wicked priests."

4. Alexander Jannaeus

The comments on the last part of Habakkuk 2:8 state that, because of the wrong done to the Teacher of Righteousness by the Wicked Priest, God delivered him "into the hand of his enemies, afflicting him with a destroying scourge, in bitterness of soul, because he acted wickedly against his elect." Alexander Jannaeus (103-76 B.C.) is described by Josephus (*Antiquities of the Jews,* xiii, 3:5) as barely escaping with his life after being pushed into a deep ravine while fighting Obedas, an Arab king. Several writers think that the passage in the Habakkuk Commentary refers to that episode.

Alexander Jannaeus was hated by the populace. Josephus records an episode which took place at the Feast of Tabernacles. Alexander was about to officiate at the altar, when the people in a body rose up and pelted him with citrons and palm-branches which they had brought with them for the celebration of the feast. They shouted insults at him. Jannaeus ordered a massacre of the people and he and the Pharisees remained on bitter terms until his death.

A somewhat similar experience is recorded in the Habakkuk Commentary (on 2:15) where we read that the Wicked Priest "persecuted the Teacher of Righteousness in order to confound him by a display of violent temper, wishing to banish him; and at the time of their festival of rest, the day of Atonement, he appeared to them to confuse them and to make them stumble on the day of fasting, their sabbatical rest."

The attack on the feast of Tabernacles, described by Josephus, resulted in a persecution of the Pharisees. The attack on the Day of Atonement, mentioned in the Habakkuk Commentary, evidently involved the Teacher of Righteousness and his followers. There is no direct relation between the two attacks, but it is conceivable that they were both associated with the same individual.

5. Aristobulus II and Hyrcanus II

In the comments on Habakkuk 2:7-8, reference is made to "the last priests of Jerusalem, who amassed wealth and booty by plundering the people, but at the end of days, their wealth with their plunder will be delivered into the hand of the army of the Kittim . . ." In accord with the identification of the Kittim with the Romans, Josephus tells us of tribute paid by Aristobulus II to the Roman General Scaurus at Damascus in 65 B.C., and to Pompey his successor. After conquering Jerusalem (63 B.C.) tribute of 10,000 talents was demanded from the citizens, much of it probably coming from the Sadducean priests. Crassus stole 2,000 talents from the Temple in 54 B.C. While "the last priests of Jerusalem" are probably to be differentiated from the Wicked Priest, they may help us to reconstruct the period discussed in the commentary.

6. Early Roman – "The House of Absalom"

Habakkuk 1:13b reads, "Why dost thou look on faithless men, and art silent when the wicked swallows up the man more righteous than he?" The commentary explains, "This means the house of Absalom and the men of their party, who kept silence when charges were leveled against the Teacher of Righteousness and did not help him against the man of the lie, who rejected the law in the midst of their whole congregation."

To Dupont-Sommer the reference to Absalom provides a key to the historical period under discussion. He takes the name Absalom literally, and identifies this Absalom with an individual of that name who was taken prisoner by the Romans in 63 B.C. at the time Jerusalem was taken. He was uncle and father-in-law of Aristobulus II. According to Dupont-Sommer, the commentator reproaches him because, although his house was closely associated with the royal house, he did nothing to try to rescue the Teacher of Righteousness.

In view of the fact that other personages are discussed in veiled language it would seem strange if Absalom should be clearly identified. This is particularly true when we think of Absalom, David's son, and the revolt which he instigated, as providing an apt metaphor for treachery. The "house of Absalom" of the Habakkuk Commentary gave at least passive assistance to the enemies of the Teacher of Righteousness.

Although not agreeing with Dupont-Sommer's identification of Absalom, many scholars are of the opinion that the Habakkuk Commentary describes the history of the Jewish people immediately prior to the capture of Jerusalem by the Romans in 63 B.C. It is then dated in the early Roman period.

7. Ebionite

The Habakkuk Commentary describes the members of the Qumran community as "poor" (Heb. *'ebionim*). A sect of Jewish-Christians was known as "Ebionite." J. L. Teicher of Cambridge University has taken this as a clue to the identification of the Qumran community.

The Ebionites accepted Jesus as their Messiah but they continued to observe the commandments of the Mosaic law – circumcision, dietary restrictions, fasts and feasts. Essentially they were a Jewish sect which recognized Jesus as Messiah. The criticism of Jerome that "by wishing to be both Jews and Christians (they) are neither one nor the other" is, in a degree at least, justified.

To Teicher, the Qumran documents are Judeo-Christian documents. The Teacher of Righteousness is Jesus. The Wicked Priest, according to Teicher's view is the apostle Paul! The Ebionites regarded Paul as a false apostle and traitor to the

Gospel because he carried the Gospel to the Gentiles and did not require the Gentile converts to submit to the Jewish law.

In addition to the absence of any direct reference to Christianity or the person and ministry of Jesus, the archaeological evidence argues against this identification. The history of the Qumran community, according to the evidence of archaeology, ended shortly before the destruction of Jerusalem (A.D. 70). The Ebionites were making their way from Jerusalem to Pella in Transjordan at that time. Fleeing members of the Qumran community might well have influenced groups like the Ebionites but the nature of the scrolls and the evidence for their earlier date argue against Teicher's view.

D. The Teacher of Righteousness and Jesus.

Sober scholars challenge the statement of Dupont-Sommer that "the Galilean Master . . . appears in many respects as an astonishing re-incarnation of the Teacher of Righteousness." John Allegro's assertion that the Teacher of Righteousness was handed over by Alexander Jannaeus to Gentile mercenaries to be crucified, has not been validated by textual evidence. If it were so validated it would be an example of martyrdom. Christianity finds its life in the Person of Christ, and apart from that Person there would be no Christianity. While we have ample evidence of the respect paid to the Teacher of Righteousness by the Qumran community, it was possible for Philo, Josephus, and Pliny to write at length concerning the Essenes without so much as an allusion to him.

It can be said to the credit of Dupont-Sommer that in his second series of studies on the scrolls, *The Jewish Sect of Qumran and the Essenes* (pp. 161-162) he shows that there are contrasts which can be drawn between Jesus and the Teacher of Righteousness. The Teacher of Righteousness was a Levitical priest, but Jesus was a son of David. The Teacher of Righteousness probably lived in Judea most of his life, but Jesus spent most of his years in Galilee. The Teacher of Righteousness, to judge from the rules which govern the Qumran community, was a strict ascetic. Jesus mingled freely among men and was called "a winebibber" because of his associations with "publicans and sinners."

Similarities of course occur. All who teach virtue instead of vice have much in common. All who teach with the background of Scripture have much in common. All who live in the same age (Jesus and the Teacher of Righteousness are separated in time by, presumably, about a century) have a common fund of language and institutions from which to draw. The teachings of Jesus have been compared with the sayings of ancient rabbis. Jesus drew from his Jewish background and the Christian church has ever regarded Old Testament and New Testament as alike the Word of God.

III. The War Scroll

Among the discoveries at Cave 1, Qumran, purchased by E. L. Sukenik for the Hebrew University, is the well-preserved scroll containing the description of a war, real or ideal, between the righteous and the wicked. From the words of the first line of the text, Sukenik called this scroll, "The War Between the Children of Light and the Children of Darkness." Scholars designate it as 1QM, Cave 1, Qumran, *Milhamah* (the Hebrew word for war). It is popularly referred to simply as the War Scroll. It contains nineteen columns of writing and is nine and one-half feet long and six and one-quarter inches high. The scroll is well-preserved except for the lower edge which is worn, and eaten away.

Attempts have been made to locate the battle described in the War Scroll in ancient history. Some have seen the Wars of the Maccabees, others events in the time of Alexander Jannaeus, and still others events in the middle of the first century before Christ. A growing number of scholars is of the opinion that the battle here envisioned did not deal with a contemporary foe of the Qumran community, but rather with foes foreseen as oppressing the people of God in the last age, before the establishment of the Messianic kingdom. To members of the Qumran community this battle must have seemed immanent.

A. The Children of Light.

The scroll identifies the children of light as the Jews of the tribes of Levi, Judah, and Benjamin. The mention of Levi indicates the respect which members of the Qumran community had for the priesthood, a fact clearly indicated in the other sectarian scrolls. Judah and Benjamin were the tribes of the southern kingdom which had remained true to the Davidic line and had resisted the inroads of idolatry somewhat more effectively than their brethren to the north. The Qumran community clearly thought of itself as the true Israel and looked askance at the less orthodox brethren who called themselves Jews.

THE SHRINE OF THE SCROLLS on the campus of Hebrew University. The white cupola and the black basalt wall represent the battle between the Sons of Light and the Sons of Darkness described in the Qumran War Scroll, one of the scrolls preserved in the shrine. Courtesy, Israel Information Services

THE DOME OF THE SHRINE, with the cylinder containing the Book of Isaiah from Qumran, Cave I. Courtesy, Israel Information Services

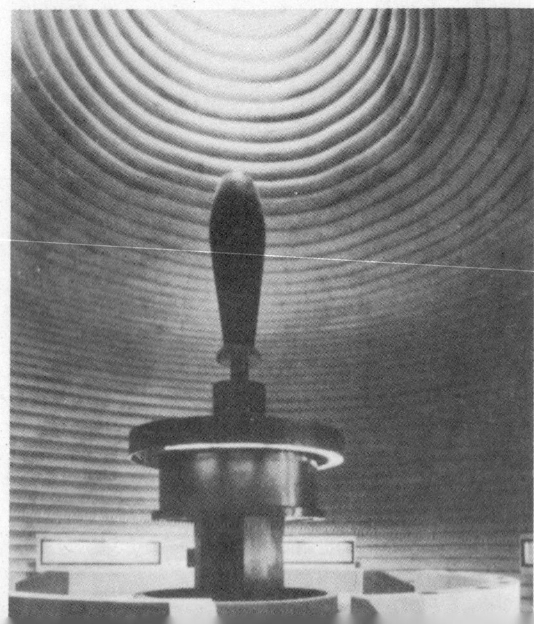

WRITING TABLES from Qumran. Courtesy, Archaeological Museum, Jerusalem

EXHIBIT OF DEAD SEA SCROLLS from the shrine at Hebrew University. Courtesy, Israel Information Services

B. The Children of Darkness.

The children of darkness, on the other hand, are identified as "the troop of Edom and Moab and the Ammonites . . . Philistia and the troops of the *Kittim* of Assyria" (1:1-2). Who are the *Kittim* of Assyria? Scholars do not feel it necessary to identify the Kittim of the War Scroll with the Kittim of the Habakkuk Commentary. In both cases they are enemies of Israel, but the positive identification of the enemy may differ in differing contexts. Reference is made in the War Scroll to the "Kittim of Egypt" as well as the "Kittim of Assyria." If these two groups of enemies of Israel are to be identified with the successors of Alexander the Great we should expect to read of Syria instead of Assyria. The Seleucids of Syria and the Ptolemies of Egypt succeeded Alexander.

There is warrant for interpreting Assyria as Syria from ancient writings. The Book of Jubilees says, "Abram journeyed from Haran, and he took Sarai his wife and Lot, his brother Haran's son to the land of Canaan; and he came to Assyria and proceeded to Shechem, and dwelt near a lofty oak" (13:1). As Millar Burrows points out, "Assyria" in this context, is somewhere between Haran and Canaan, and might very well mean Syria. Unless we take the "Kittim of Assyria" as a cryptic reference to some power known to the Qumran community but purposely veiled in the War Scroll, it seems wise to identify the "Kittim of Assyria" with the Syrians. Hellenism would then be deemed the foe, which found its ultimate expression in Antiochus Epiphanes. The evil powers are assisted by Belial and the forces of darkness and wickedness.

Recent studies, however, suggest that the War Scroll was written during the early days of the Roman occupation of Judea. Yadin, who has edited the War Scroll for the Hebrew University, claims to find echoes of Roman army strategy in the scroll. The Roman administration of Syria, and the Roman forces in Egypt become the Kittim of Assyria and Egypt, respectively according to this view.

C. The Assured Victory.

The assurance of victory is declared in the beginning of the scroll. We are not given a picture of a battle of which the outcome is uncertain, but rather of a battle which will "be a time of salvation for the people of God, and a time of dominion for all the men of his lot, but eternal destruction for all the lot of Belial" (1:5). The battle will be fought, we are told, "when the exiles of the sons of light return from the desert of the peoples to encamp in the desert of Jerusalem" (1:3). The victory of the "sons of light" will be complete. "There shall be no survivor of the sons of darkness" (1:7).

The fact that victory is assured does not lessen the intensity of the struggle. After three battles in which the sons of light are victorious we are told of three battles which result in victory for the sons of darkness. The concept of victory for the wicked is, of course, true to life. The wicked often triumph for a season. It is also a literary necessity to indicate the fierceness of the battle. The forces appear evenly matched and a casual by-stander might wonder what the outcome of the battle would be.

In the "seventh turn of fortune" God intervenes in the battle so that the "sons of light" win a great victory. This, presumably, ushers in the Messianic age.

D. Battle Arrangements.

Since the "sons of light" are waging spiritual warfare, even as they fight their human enemies, considerable attention is given to the technical matters of battle-formation and ritual. The army is divided into groups of 1000, 100, 50, and 10, with captains over each detachment. This appears to be a clear reference to Old Testament organization. The large numbers, in contrast to the relatively small Qumran community, have suggested that the plan of battle was ideal and eschatological.

Soldiers are classified according to age: Cavalry (30-40 years); Officers (40-50 years) and Commanders (50-60 years). The youths of 25-30 years are classified as common soldiers (7:1-15).

E. The Trumpets.

The trumpets are inscribed with identifying insignia such as, "The Princes of God," "The Order of God," "The Called of God," and "The Chiefs of the Fathers of the Congregation." The "trumpets of breaking camp" are inscribed with the words, "The Powers of God for scattering the enemy and putting to flight those who hate righteousness and turning back kindness against those who hate God." The "trumpets of pursuit" bear the words, "God's smiting of all the Sons of Darkness – His anger will not turn back until they are destroyed." The trumpets of "the way of the return from battle" contain the words, "The rejoicings of God at the return of peace" (3:1-11).

F. The Standards.

The standards, or battle flags, also contain inscriptions designed to encourage the faithful and strike terror into the hearts of their enemies. One of them bears the words, "The anger of God with fury against Belial and all the men of His lot without remnant," and, another, "The position of the wicked has ceased by the power of God" (4:1-14).

In going into battle the "sons of light" carry banners reading, "The Truth of God," "The Righteousness of God," "The Glory of God," and "The Justice of God." Each group has its appropriate banner for each experience in battle. In the thick of the battle, one group unfurls a banner reading, "The Destruction of God on every nation of vanity." Returning from victorious combat banners such as "The Deliverances of God," "The Victory of God," and "The Peace of God" can be read (4:1-14).

G. The Prayers of the Priests.

The prayer of the priests is, to a large degree, instrumental in bringing victory in battle. Before entering combat, the priest prays,

> Arise, O warrior; take thy captives, O glorious man!
> Seize thy plunder, O doer of mighty deeds!
> Lay thy hand on the necks of thy enemies
> And thy foot on the heaps of the slain;
> smite the nations; thy adversaries,
> and may thy sword devour guilty flesh!
> Fill thy land with glory,
> And thine inheritance with blessing!
> [Let there be] a multitude of possessions in thy fields,
> silver and gold and precious stones in thy palaces.
> Rejoice greatly, O Zion;
> Shine forth with shouts of joy, O Jerusalem;
> and exult, ye cities of Judah!
> Let thy gates be continually open,
> that the wealth of nations may be brought unto thee;
> and let their kings serve thee,
> and all thy oppressors bow down to thee
> and lick the dust of thy feet.
> O daughters of my people, cry aloud with songs of joy;
> Adorn yourselves with glorious ornaments (12:10-15).

After victory, the priests utter their psalm of thanksgiving in the words:

> Blessed be the God of Israel
> Who is faithful to his covenant

and to the testimonies of salvation
for the people whom He redeemed.

* * *

For we are thy people,
For thy faithful deeds we praise thy Name
and for thy mighty acts we exalt (thee).

* * *

Be highly exalted, O God of gods,
And be lifted up in thy wrath. (14:4-16)

H. Dualism.

An interesting by-product of the study of the War Scroll is the renewed interest in the study of dualism as a theological and historical concept. As is well known, John's Gospel speaks of the antagonism between light and darkness, truth and error. These concepts have frequently been ascribed to the impact of Greek philosophical speculation on early Christianity. This was taken by many as proof that the Gospel of John was late in date and non-Jewish in theological orientation.

This ethical dualism, once thought to be of non-Jewish importation into the thought of the early church, is now seen to be in pre-Christian Jewish thought. John's terminology is now known to be similar to that used by Jews long before the earliest New Testament writings. Rowley suggests a Maccabean date for the composition of the War Scroll. Yadin dates it in the early Roman period. It certainly originated in a period of intense opposition to a power which threatened the very existence of Israel. Even though we consider the battles described in the scroll as eschatological, they had a historical context. The War Scroll offers incontrovertible proof that ethical dualism had entered Hebrew vocabulary before the Christian period. That Jesus made use of that vocabulary in discussing spiritual reality is evidenced by the New Testament gospels, particularly John.

Many writers feel that Iranian influences were strong in the Qumran Community. Since Zoroastrianism posits a conflict between Ahura Mazda (the god of light, truth, and goodness) and Ahriman (the god of darkness, error, and evil), a ready explanation for the theology of the War Scroll has been seen. The Jews, of course, were settled in the Persian Empire for a considerable period of time, some of them returning to Jerusalem at the time of the decree of Cyrus, but many remaining in the East.

While recognizing Iranian influence on Jewish thinking, as well as influence from every nation with which Israel came in contact, we have already noted that dualism is much older in ancient near-eastern thought than the period of Zoroaster. In the Bible itself, Moses and the magicians of Egypt, Elijah and the prophets of Baal represent a real ethical dualism. The Bible, however, asserts that Yahweh is all powerful. Although he may permit the forces of evil to triumph temporarily (for reasons which puzzled ancient Israel as much as they puzzle us), ultimately His kingdom will be established and every foe vanquished. This is the message of the War Scroll as it is of the canonical Scriptures.

Another error we must avoid is that of assuming that Christianity uncritically adopted the ideas of Essenism, or of the Qumran community. If the Gospel of John may be compared with the War Scroll, it may also be contrasted. The emphasis on priesthood, rites and ceremonies which we find in the War Scroll is missing from John. In place of a boasting in legal righteousness, so characteristic of the Qumran community, John emphasizes the grace of God in Christ as the only salvation for lost mankind. Qumran boasted a Teacher of Righteousness. John wrote of a Savior from sin.

IV. The Thanksgiving Scroll

The Thanksgiving Scroll (Hebrew, *Hodayoth*) is in two parts. The part which was first opened contained three sheets, each with four columns of text. They are about thirteen inches high, and contain as many as thirty-nine lines of writing to a column. The second part was a crumpled mass of about seventy fragments by the time it reached the hands of Sukenik and the other scholars at the Hebrew University. Much of the leather of the scroll is very dark brown, and some of it has become black due to the ravages of time. Infra-red photography has enabled scholars to read some previously illegible sections.

Two principal hands can be recognized in the writing of the scroll and the section known through the fragments. From this fact it has been concluded that the middle of the scroll has been preserved in good condition, and that the beginning and the end of the scroll is represented by the fragments.

The Thanksgiving Scroll is a collection of psalms expressing the views and feelings of an Israelite who may have been associated with the Qumran community. The style is an imitation of the Biblical Psalms. The majority begin with the phrase, "I

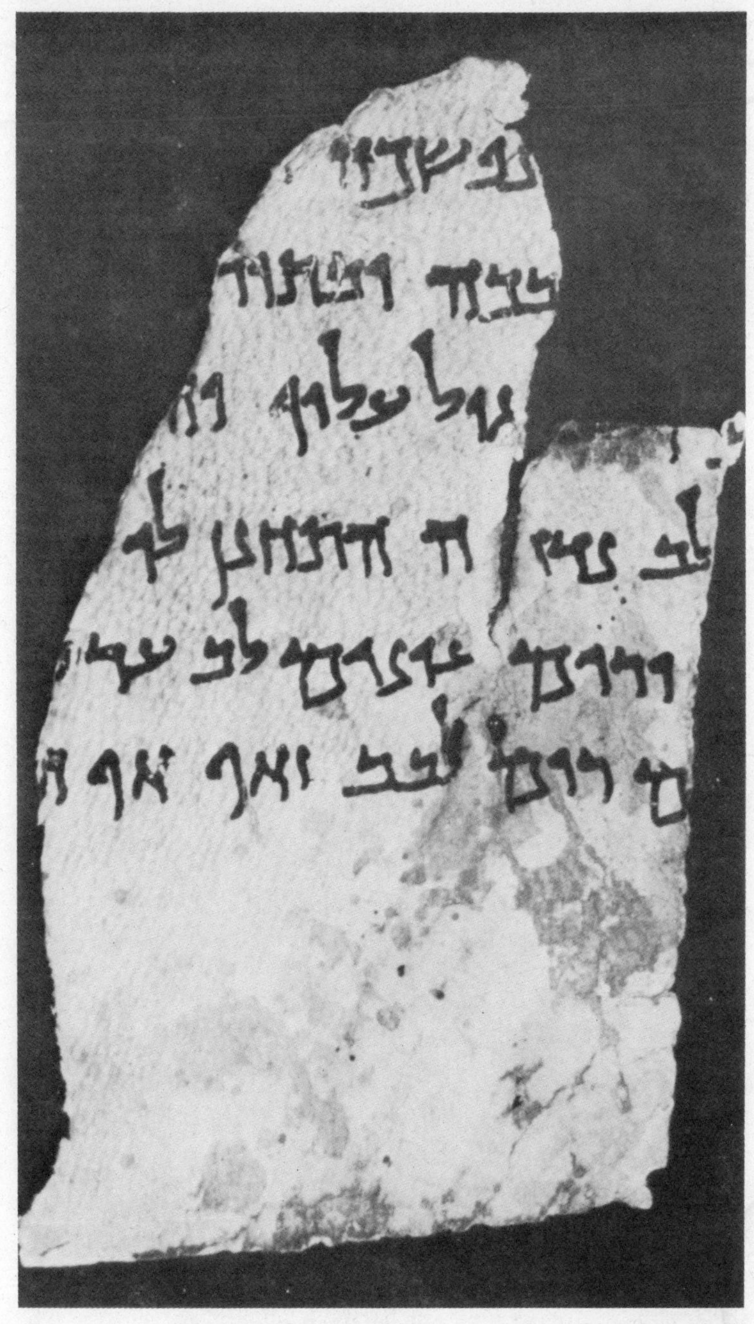

PARCHMENT FRAGMENT of a scroll of non-Biblical Psalms discovered at Qumran. Courtesy, Oriental Institute, The University of Chicago.

thank thee, God," which caused Dr. Sukenik, their first editor, to call the scroll, The Thanksgiving Scroll. About thirty-five whole and fragmentary Thanksgiving Psalms have survived.

The psalms are of a distinctively personal nature. Psalm number seven (4:8-37) presents the writer as the recipient of special revelation from God.

He has bitter enemies:

> For they have become loathsome to themselves,
> and do not regard me though thou dost show thy power through me;
> but they drive me from my land like a bird from its nest,
> and all my neighbors and friends are driven far from me.
> They have regarded me as a broken vessel.
> But they are preachers of lies and prophets of deceit.
> They plotted mischief against me,
> exchanging thy law which thou didst engrave in my heart,
> for smooth things for thy people.

He is assured that God will bring judgment upon these who have resisted God's word and His messenger:

> But thou, O God, wilt answer them,
> judging them in thy power
>
> . . . .
>
> Thou wilt cut off in judgment all men of deceit,
> and prophets of error will be found no more . . .

God has vindicated his servant, however, and given him numerous followers and a wide ministry:

> By me thou hast enlightened the faces of many,
> and hast shown thy power through me countless times.
> Thou hast made known unto me thy wondrous mysteries,
> and in thy wondrous company thou hast shown forth thy power.
> Thou hast wrought wondrously in the presence of many,
> for the sake of thy glory . . .

The statement, "They drive me from my land like a bird from its nest," corresponds to the statement in the Habakkuk Commentary that the Wicked Priest drove the Teacher of Righteousness into exile. This fact, with the allusions to the writer of the psalm as a persecuted teacher with numerous followers who flock to listen to his teaching, has caused Sukenik and others to conclude that the Teacher of Righteousness is the author of this Psalm, and perhaps others. Dupont-Sommer thinks that a devoted disciple may have written the psalm in honor of the Teacher of Righteousness, mystically assuming his personality.

V. The Temple Scroll

During the Six Days War of June, 1967, Yigael Yadin of the Hebrew University acquired an impressive scroll which has been tentatively entitled The Temple Scroll. The existence of this ancient document had been known since the early 1960's, but the Arab owners were reluctant to part with it. They knew the price paid for such material, and were apparently awaiting the moment when a very high price would be paid. In the meantime the scroll had begun to deteriorate, and Yadin feels that his prompt action in taking the scroll has preserved it for the world of scholarship. The actual circumstances under which the scroll was acquired are still not known. Yadin is seeking to keep them from public knowledge for fear they might compromise the possible of the acquisition of other material in the future.

Two weeks after the war, Yadin invited J. Shenhav, who had been chief technical advisor with the excavations at Hazor and Masada, to assist him in unrolling the scroll. Due to its age and deterioration, this proved to be a monumental task.

The scroll was tightly rolled, with many pieces peeled off and detached. The upper part was badly mutilated, and its brown-black appearance reminded Yadin of melted chocolate. The lower part was intact, and it represented many rolled layers to a diameter of about two inches.

The aim of the scholars was to unroll the scroll without further damage. They decided to expose it to a high degree of humidity, and then to refrigerate it for several minutes. The freezing congealed the surface matter, while leaving the membranes limp enough to be manipulated. Because the scroll was so tightly rolled, sometimes the humidity caused the ink of the Hebrew letters to come off on the back of the piece of parchment to which it had been stuck. It was then a simple matter to photograph the letters which were reversed, and then to reverse the negatives to make final prints. Undetachable fragments from the scroll were subjected to infra-red, ultra-violet, or x-ray photography in an effort to reconstruct the text.

As this laborious project came to an end, Yadin had the entire text photographed on prints the size of the original sheets. Then he had them stapled together to form a continuous scroll which could be rolled up like the original. As reconstructed, the scroll extends twenty-eight feet, comprising sixty-six columns of text, about half of which is in excellent condition. A full column has twenty lines of text. Parts of the first sheet are missing, and the earliest columns suffered the most damage. About two-thirds of the scroll can be easily read by Hebrew scholars.

Yadin has no doubt that the scroll is from the Qumran area. Palaeography – the form of the letters – suggests that it was written during Herodian times (i.e., from the middle of the first century B.C. to the middle of the first century of the Christian era). It could not have been written later than A.D. 70 when the Roman Tenth Legion occupied the Qumran settlement.

The calendar followed in the Temple Scroll is that used by the Qumran sectarian community and other apocalyptic groups within the Jewish community. The calendar comprised twelve months of thirty days each, with an additional day at the end of each three month period, or 364 days in all. This produced a year of exactly fifty-two weeks. The first day of the first month always fell on a Wednesday.

Vocabulary also indicates that the scroll was written during the latter part of the Second Temple period, i.e. within a century or so of the destruction of Jerualem by the armies of Titus (A.D. 70). Post-biblical Hebrew words frequently have parallels in the Mishna.

The scroll is written in the style of a law addressed to Moses by God Himself. As such it is evidently meant to rank with the Biblical texts themselves. God speaks, in the first person, and His law (Hebrew, Torah) is binding upon all. The divine Name (the tetragammaton, YHWH) is written in the same script as the remainder of the scroll, like the Qumran Biblical texts. In non-Biblical texts an archaic script known as Paleo-Hebrew is usually used in writing the sacred Name.

A. Statutes of the Kings

A major portion of the scroll is devoted to matters of practical defense. Unlike the War Scroll, which describes an idealized eschatological battle in which the forces of Yahweh prevail over the forces of the wicked, the Temple Scroll offers counsel on preparing defenses against enemies which threaten Israel with annihilation in historical times. The king's bodyguard is to be mobilized to protect the king and his wives day and night "lest they fall into the hands of the gentiles." The bodyguard comprises 12,000 soldiers, one thousand from each of the twelve tribes, "men of truth," "god-fearing," "hating unjust gain."

When the king hears of a threat to the nation, he is instructed to mobilize one-tenth of the people. If the enemy is numerous and powerful, one-fifth of the people must be called up. If the enemy advances with a large number of horses and chariots, one-third of the people should prepare for battle, while two-thirds remain to protect the frontiers and the cities.

When the war actually begins the population is equally divided, half engaged in battle, and half defending the cities. Any man who betrays the people of Israel by passing information to the enemy is killed for his treachery. The king is rewarded or punished, depending on his obedience to the law of Yahweh here presented as "my law" in the Temple Scroll.

B. Sacrifices and Feasts

The scroll describes the observances of Succoth (Tabernacles), Passover, and the Day of Atonement in considerable detail. Following the description of Shavuoth (Pentecost), fifty days after Passover when the first fruits were offered (Exodus 23: 16), we read of the Feast of New Wine, fifty days after Shavuoth, and the Feast of New Oil, fifty days later. These feasts are based on the sectarian calendar used in Jewish apocalyptic circles. Techniques for sacrifices and observance of the feasts are described in the scroll. Regulations are more rigid than those later codified in the Mishna. The author of the Temple Scroll, and those who accepted it as God's Word, felt that sacrifice and Temple should exist, but in a way consistent with the sect's distinctive teachings.

Religious Laws

Among the laws for ritual purification in cases of uncleanness, some parallel those of the Mishna, while others differ by being more strict. Regarding a pregnant (lit. "full") woman whose embryo has died in her womb, the Temple Scroll says, "All the days that it remains inside her she is as unclean as a tomb." The woman is regarded as unclean because, like a tomb, she has a dead person within her. The Mishna, on the other hand, states, "The mother remains clean until the child comes forth." The mother is ceremonially unclean only when her body rejects the dead embryo – after which, of course, she undergoes rites of purification.

We also find laws in the Temple Scroll that appear neither in the Bible nor in the Mishna. The dead are not to be buried within the house, but in a specially designated cemetery outside the city. In order to conserve space we find the stipulation that four cities should share one burial plot: "Thou shalt not follow the laws of the gentiles who bury their dead inside their houses; and thou shalt fix a special place for each four cities to bury their dead."

For the contemporary scholar, the main interest in the Temple Scroll is this material which is not in the Biblical Pentateuch. Its sectarian, polemical nature enhances our picture of the life of the Jewish community at the time of Christ.

C. The Temple

Almost half of the scroll contains detailed instructions for the building and furnishing of the Temple, paralleling the Biblical description of the Tabernacle (Exodus 35-40). This was evidently written to supply a missing law for the building of the Temple. In I Chronicles 28:19 we read that David gave to his son Solomon the directions for building the Temple, made clear "by the writing from the hand of the Lord concerning it, all the work to be done according to the plan." The writer of this scroll, aware of the inspired directions for building the Tabernacle, and convinced of the sanctity of the Temple, wrote what he thought to be God's Word concerning the building of the perfect Temple.

The description does not follow the plans of Solomon's Temple, or that of the Temple built by Zerubbabel after the return from exile, or of Herod's Temple which was standing at the time the scroll was written. The author believed in a future eschatological Temple which God Himself would build, but he also believed that man should build such an ideal Temple now according to the divinely-revealed plans.

The historical Temple, like the Tabernacle before it, had two courts, an outer and an inner court. The Temple Scroll adds a middle court, making three in all. Each court is square and the three are arranged so that they are concentric. The inner court has sides of 250 cubits each, the middle court 500 cubits, and the outer court 1600 cubits. Chambers are provided for priests and Levites.

For the first time we learn that booths were erected in the Temple itself during Succoth (The Feast of Tabernacles). The scroll suggests that booths were provided for the heads of the Israelite tribes.

The tribes are also commemorated in the names of the twelve gates, three on each side, which provided access to the middle and the outer court of the Temple. The Biblical Book of the Revelation speaks of twelve gates to the holy city, each of which bore the name of one of the tribes (Revelation 21: 12).

D. Rules of Cleanliness

Matters of personal and public hygiene, including sexual matters, are given consideration in the Scroll. Lepers and the lame were restricted to especially built places around the city. They were not permitted to approach the Temple area.

Public toilets were to be built about fifteen hundred yards northwest of the Temple, near the present site of the American School of Oriental Research. The reason for this appears to be geographical. To the east is the Mount of Olives, holy in its own right and higher than the Temple, hence visible. The west would not be suitable because the prevailing winds come from that direction. To the south are hills which the Temple mount overlooks. The northwest was ideal for providing conveniences which could not be seen from the Temple area.

Work on the Temple Scroll has just begun. Yigael Yadin's preliminary reports, however, provide evidence that this important scroll will challenge Semitic scholarship for a good many years to come. Like the Manual of Discipline, it will give insight into the beliefs of an important community of Jews at the time of Christ and the beginnings of Christianity.

VI. The Copper Scroll.

Considerable interest was aroused by preliminary reports concerning the two copper rolls which were found in Cave 3, Qumran, in March, 1952. Originally one sheet, an accident evidently caused the break which has produced our two rolls.

A significant quotation from the scroll appeared in the public press: "In the cistern which is below the rampart on the east side, in a place hollowed out of rock; 600 bars of silver . . . Close by, below the southern corner of the portico at Zadok's tomb and underneath the pilaster in the exedras, a vessel of incense in pine wood, and a vessel of incense in cassia wood . . . In the pit near by toward the north, near the grave, in a hole opening to the north, there is a copy of this book with explanations, measurements, and all details" (*TIME*, June 11, 1956).

Why a community which had renounced this world's goods to go into the desert to "prepare the way of the Lord" should be concerned with such mundane affairs remains a puzzle. The story of the decipherment of the Copper Scroll and its contents is given in John Marco Allegro's book, *The Treasure of the Copper Scroll* (London: 1960).

VII. The Genesis Apocryphon

Because of its poor state of preservation and the fact that a purchaser could not be obtained, the so-called "Lamech scroll" was literally a closed book to the world of scholarship until February 1956. With the purchase of the scrolls by the Israeli government, serious efforts were made to unroll it. Under the supervision of two Hebrew University professors, Nachman Avi-

THE COPPER SCROLLS as they were discovered in Cave 3. Courtesy, Palestine Archaeological Museum.

gad and Yigdael Yadin, the unrolling was achieved by a German expert, Professor James Biberkraut.

It was found that this scroll did not contain the lost Book of Lamech, as scholars at first suggested, but rather an Aramaic paraphrase of chapters 5 to 15 of the Book of Genesis, making use of legends which were current among the Jews in antiquity. Its study provides insights into the ways in which the Biblical account of Genesis was understood, interpreted, and embellished by these ancient Bible-loving people.

The scroll was originally about nine feet long with eighteen pages of manuscript. The beginning and the end are missing. Three pages are complete, containing 34 lines of text. One page is nearly complete and five pages contain considerable portions of the original. Others contain a few lines or single words. The handwriting may be compared with that of the War Scroll.

In a style somewhat reminiscent of the *Book of Jubilees* the author has given an interesting description of Sarah's beauty in discussing the section dealing with the taking of Sarah by the Pharaoh of Egypt (Genesis 12). In discussing Lot's departure (Genesis 13) an extended version of verses 14-18 gives us a rich and original explanation of the topography of the land. The treatment of Genesis 14 is full of names and places which differ from known versions. Nahman, Arigad and Yigael Yadin edited the Genesis Apocryphon (Magnes Press, Jerusalem, 1956).

6

THE IDENTITY OF THE QUMRAN SECT

Shortly after the discovery of the Qumran scrolls, scholars began to note similarities between the Essenes as described by Josephus, Philo, and Pliny and the community of the scrolls. The majority of the scholars classify the Qumran community as Essene, or near-Essene. Others have pointed out parallels with the Pharisees, Sadducees, Zealots, Ebionites, and other groups.

Both the Qumran sect and the Essenes were groups which had separated themselves from the "normative" Judaism of their day, including the temple services. Each had rules of discipline. A superintendent, or overseer was responsible for the life of members of each. Possessions were held in common, both at Qumran and among the Essenes. A newcomer had to undergo a period of probation, and the uninitiated were excluded from the common meal in both groups. Ritual washing was practiced among the Essenes and at Qumran.

On the other hand there are differences between the descriptions of the Essenes as given in Josephus, Philo, and Pliny and the practices of Qumran. The Essenes sent gifts of incense to the Temple, although they repudiated animal sacrifice. The attitude at Qumran was one of antipathy to the Jerusalem priesthood. The descriptions of the Essenes do not indicate the prominence of priests in that movement as do the Qumran writings for the community. There is no Teacher of Righteousness in the descriptions of the Essenes.

There are other areas where we have not yet evidence to either affirm or deny affinities. Philo speaks of the Essenes as repudiating slavery. Slavery is not mentioned at Qumran. The

Essenes wore white garments, but we have no description of the clothing of members of the Qumran community.

The sources indicate that the Essenes as a group condemn marriage. Philo is explicit here: "For no one of the Essenes marries a wife, because woman is a selfish and excessively jealous creature, and has great power to destroy the morals of man, and to mislead with continual tricks; for she is always devising flattering speeches and other kinds of hypocrisy as on a stage; bewitching the eyes and the ears; and when they are subjugated like things stultified, she proceeds to undermine the ruling intellect. But when she has children the woman becomes full of pride and arrogance, audaciously speaks out that which she previously merely indicated in treacherous disguise, and without any shame compels one to do whatever is hostile to the brotherhood; for he who is chained by the charms of a woman or cares for children by necessity of nature, is no longer the same person to others, but is entirely changed, having unawares become a slave instead of a free man" (*Apology for the Jews,* preserved in Eusebius, *Praep Evang.*, viii, 11, quoted in C. D. Ginsburg, *The Essenes*).

On the other hand, Josephus writes, "Moreover, there is another order of Essenes, who agree with the rest as to their way of living, and customs, and laws, but differ from them in the point of marriage, as thinking that by not marrying they cut off the principal part of human life, which is the prospect of succession; nay, rather, that if all men should be of the same opinion, the whole race of mankind would fail. However, they try their spouses for three years, and if they find that they have their natural purgations thrice, as trials that they are likely to be fruitful, they then actually marry them. But they do not use to accompany with their wives when they are with child, as a demonstration that they do not marry out of regard to pleasure, but for the sake of posterity. Now the women go into the baths with some of their garments on, as the men do with somewhat girded about them. And thus are the customs of this order of Essenes" (*Wars of the Jews* ii, 8:13).

These two quotations indicate that in something as basic as the attitude toward marriage, communities that considered themselves as Essenes held different viewpoints. It is possible to point out differences in the Qumran scrolls themselves. These may indicate differences which may be accounted for by the historical development of the sect. They may also reflect differences in attitudes and practices among related groups. Evidently the term Essene was broad enough in meaning to include various groups of monastic or semi-monastic nature which differed among themselves in certain details. Josephus classified the religious life of his people in three "philosophies" – Pharisees, Sadducees, and Essenes. If this classification is accepted, the Qumran community appears to fit into the third group. On the other hand, Josephus appears to have over-simplified the complex religious situation of his day.

The geographical reference to the Essenes in the writings of Pliny the Elder (*Historica Naturalis* 5:17) is one of the strongest evidences for identifying them with the Qumran community. He says that they lived "on the west side away from the shores" of the Dead Sea. "Below them lay En Gedi, a town once second only to Jerusalem in its fertility and groves of palms." An objection can be raised, however, in that Pliny insists that the Essenes were celibates, and the evidence of the appendix to the Manual of Discipline and the Qumran cemetery indicates that the community was one of marrying Essenes. Since the geographical reference fits Qumran, and only Qumran, it seems best to resolve the difficulty by the recognition of possibilities of change within the Qumran community and the recognition that Pliny's information about the Essenes may have come from an outside source which was ignorant of the marrying Essenes.

As has been indicated, scholarship has not been unanimous in identifying the Qumran community as Essene. Saul Lieberman has pointed out comparisons between the Qumran community and the Phariasaic *ḥaburah* – Pharisaic societies whose membership undertook to observe strictly the laws of ritual purity. M. H. Gottstein has suggested an "anti-Essene polemic" in the Qumran scrolls, contrasting the Qumran emphasis on obedience to the law with the Essene emphasis on ceremonial purity. The ancient writers, however, are unanimous in their praise of the Essenes for their high morality. To dismiss them as empty ritualists does not appear to do them justice.

Teicher's view that the Qumran community is to be identified with the Ebionites of early Christian history has been refuted by the evidence of archaeology. The age and contents of the scroll indicate a pre-Christian origin.

While it is wise to counsel caution, the preponderance of evidence indicates that the members of the Qumran community were marrying Essenes.

7

THE ESSENES AND CHRISTIANITY

Since the time of Renan, who termed Christianity "an Essenism which succeeded on a big scale" scholars have been intrigued with the thought of Essene influence on Christ, John the Baptist, and Christianity as a whole. Similarities have frequently been pointed out between the life of an Essene community and the life of the early church. There is the danger, however, of overlooking the differences which also exist. The contrasts frequently appear more significant than the comparisons.

I. Jesus and Essenism

It should be observed that there is nothing derogatory to the person of Christ in the assumption that He or His followers were of Essene background. The Scriptures make it clear that the mother of our Lord was a Jewess, and that He became incarnate in the midst of a Jewish environment. If it were proved that this environment was also Essene, Christian theology would lose nothing and the uniqueness of Jesus would be no more disproved than it is disproved by the assertion of the Jewish origin of Jesus after the flesh. Dr. Christian David Ginsburg boldly asserts that all Jews in the time of Christ were either Pharisees, Sadducees, or Essenes, and that, since Jesus clearly did not fit into one of the first two categories he must be ranked among the third. Proof of this statement, however, is lacking. If Jesus is to be ranked with the Essenes it must be on the basis of better evidence.

As a matter of fact, the life and teaching of Jesus present striking contrasts to what we know of Essenism. The Essenes were thorough-going legalists who, according to Josephus were "more scrupulous than any other Jews" regarding sabbath observance. Jesus, while obedient to the law, clearly taught "It is lawful to do well on the sabbath day" (Matthew 22:1-12).

The Zadokite work indicates the ultimate in sabbath observance. Among the prohibitions is the following: "Let no man assist a beast in birth on the Sabbath day. Even if she drops (her new-born young) into a cistern or a pit, let him not keep it (the young) alive on the Sabbath" (14:36). With this may be contrasted the words of Jesus, "What man shall there be among you, that shall have one sheep, and if it fall into a pit on the sabbath day, will he not lay hold on it, and lift it out?" (Matthew 12:11).

Jesus was not an ascetic. The Gnostic idea that matter is evil finds no echo in his words. In His own words, Jesus "came eating and drinking" and those who observed him said, "Behold a man gluttonous, and a winebibber, a friend of publicans and sinners" (Matthew 11:19). The Essenes, however, "reject pleasures as an evil." "They think that oil is a defilement; and if any one of them be anointed without his own approbation, it is wiped off his body; for they think to be sweaty is a good thing, as they do also to be clothed in white garments" (Josephus, *Wars of the Jews,* ii 8:2-3). Jesus said, "Thou, when thou fastest, anoint thy head" (Matthew 6:17).

Ceremonial lustrations are basic in Essene thinking. A daily ceremonial bath takes place before dining (Josephus, *op. cit.,* ii, 8:5). The novices, or junior members of the group are regarded as unclean so that "if the seniors should be touched by the juniors, they must wash themselves as if they had intermixed themselves with the company of a foreigner" (Josephus, *op. cit.,* ii 8:10). With this may be contrasted the words of Jesus, "Not that which goeth into the mouth defileth the man; but that which cometh out of the mouth, this defileth the man" (Matthew 15:11).

Josephus says that the Essenes send offerings to the Temple, but that they perform no sacrifices (*Antiquities* xviii 1:5). Philo says that they are "worshippers of God, yet they did not sacrifice animals, regarding a reverent mind as the only true sacrifice" (*Quod Omnis Probus Liber*). Whether or not this attitude developed among the Essenes after a rift with the Jerusalem priesthood is not immediately evident. That the Essenes were cut off from the Temple sacrifices is certain. Yet Jesus from childhood resorted to the temple. It was the scene of his teaching and miracles. He changed the cleansed lepers to go to the priests and offer the sacrifice prescribed in the law (Matthew 8:4, cf. Leviticus 14:57). He did not hesitate to upbraid the Pharisees and Sadducees for their hypocrisy, but he never condemned sacrifice and offering. By his own testimony he had come, not to destroy but to fulfill the law (Matthew 5:17).

According to Josephus, the Essenes denied the doctrine of the resurrection of the body. "For their doctrine is this: That bodies are corruptible, and that the matter they are made of is not permanent; but that the souls are immortal, and continue forever; and that they come out of the most subtle air, and are united to their bodies as in prisons, into which they are drawn by a certain natural enticement; but that when they are set free from the bonds of the flesh, they then, as released from a long bondage, rejoice and mount upward" (Josephus, *Wars of the Jews,* ii 8:11). The cornerstone of apostolic preaching was the resurrected Christ.

Much of the discussion concerning the relationship between Christianity and Essenism is based on the argument from silence. Jesus did not condemn the Essenes as he did the Pharisees and Sadducees. Therefore, we are told, he must have been friendly toward them. The relative smallness of the Essene movement, and its tendency to remove itself from the centers of Jewish life may account for this omission in the preaching of Jesus. Not only does the New Testament not mention the Essenes, the Jewish Talmud also ignores them.

II. John the Baptist and Essenism

The fact that John the Baptist preached "in the wilderness of Judea" (Matthew 3:1) had caused some to conclude that he was an Essene and that he had been a member of the Qumran community. Such statements, of course, can neither be proved nor refuted. It is certainly possible that John was acquainted with the Essenes. Jesus testified to the fact that John was an ascetic (Matthew 11:18). Terming the Pharisees and Sadducees a "generation of vipers" (Matthew 3:7-9) would probably have agreed with Essene estimates of their worth. Yet John differed from the Essenes. They were an exclusive group which never evangelized those who were deemed subject to "the spirit of error." John became an aggressive evangelist. Their ceremonial cleansings were reserved for the fully initiated. John's baptism was for the repentant soul, apart from any question of spiritual attainment. John early saw in Jesus the promised Messiah. The Qumran community, and Essenism, so far as we know, never recognized in Jesus the Messiah of whom the prophets spoke. If John ever was a member of an Essene community, he broke with it before becoming the preacher described in our gospels.

III. What Do Similarities Mean?

Points of similarity may be drawn between the teachings of Jesus and the Essenes. Both insisted that a man's word need not be re-enforced by an oath. Both taught humility and godliness. Both minimized the importance of riches and taught principles of brotherhood. In Essenism, however, it was a brotherhood of the initiated, of those who had attained a degree of spiritual perfection as demanded by the sect. In Christ it was a brotherhood which included "publicans and sinners" who were forgiven of their sins and welcomed into the family of God by His grace.

Both Essenism and Christianity had a common origin – the Scriptures of the Old Testament. That many of their ideals were similar may be accounted for by that fact.

Certain of the ideas which are associated with the Essenes also appear in the history of the early church. The concept that the body (in common with all matter) is evil is basic in Gnosticism. Asceticism leading to monasticism is another phenomenon of early church history which can be studied in this connection. Our interest, however, is with the origins of Christianity. There is no proof of Essene impact on those origins, and there is much evidence of contrast between Jesus and the Essenes in both life and teaching.

8

THE SCROLLS AND THE TEXT OF THE OLD TESTAMENT

For a long time scholars had been skeptical of ever finding ancient manuscripts of the books of the Old Testament. In the 1948 printing of Sir Frederick Kenyon's excellent book *Our Bible and the Ancient Manuscripts* he makes the statement: "There is indeed, no probability that we shall ever find manuscripts of the Hebrew text going back to a period before the formation of the text which we know as Masoretic. We can only arrive at an idea of it by a study of the earliest translations made from it. . . ." At the very time the presses were turning out copies of the book, evidence was being brought to light which would make it impossible for such sentiments to be uttered in the future.

Scholars used to console themselves with the thought that the clay tablets of Babylonia and the papyri of Egypt would help them to understand something of the Biblical backgrounds. They had abundant reason for such thoughts, for new worlds of Sumerian, Babylonian, Assyrian, Hurrian, Hittite, Canaanite, and Egyptian life and culture opened before the serious Bible student of the twentieth century. He had more than he could absorb in a lifetime. Ancient Biblical manuscripts had long since passed from the scene, and he had to expend his energies in other directions. So he thought. But the year 1947 with its discovery, among other writings, of two ancient manuscripts of Isaiah in Cave 1, Qumran, put an end to such thoughts. The Bible student still has the responsibility of learning all that he can of the literary and non-literary remains of those peoples which had contact with ancient Israel. In addition to the valuable material which a century and a half of archaeological labors have brought to our attention, however, we now have actual manuscripts of Old Testament books from the pre-Christian era – a thousand years older than previously known texts.

I. The Materials of Textual Criticism

To appreciate the significance of these recent discoveries we must have some understanding of the materials which are used by the student of the text of Scripture – Old Testament and New Testament. Since students of the New Testament text have had more comparative material with which to work than their colleagues working in the field of Old Testament, a word concerning their labors may be in order.

A. New Testament.

From the writing of the original autograph of the New Testament books to the time of the invention of printing, in the fifteenth century, the books of the New Testament, as well as all other books deemed worthy of multiplication, were carefully copied by hand. Those who copied Scripture were usually pious monks who carefully labored over the sacred text. In the earlier period the writing was in capital letters (uncials), each of which was written separately. During the ninth century a new style of Greek writing was developed, modified in shape so that words could be written continuously without lifting the pen after each letter. This new type of writing (in minuscules) made copying a much swifter process, with the result that several thousand manuscripts of the New Testament were extant by the time printing made the work of the copyist superfluous.

From among the thousands of handwritten copies, the printer had to determine the text which seemed to be the best. By "the best" we mean the one which most closely approximates the original. Careful as the copyists were, minor errors were bound to creep into their texts – errors of spelling, of omissions, of repetitions, of transpositions, of introducing marginal notes into the text – errors which in no sense affected the theology of Scripture, but errors which the careful student wished to identify and eliminate.

The first printed Greek Testament is that of the Dutch humanist, Erasmus. The first edition of Erasmus' work was based on six manuscripts, only one of which was relatively ancient, and none of which was complete. We are told that, since they did not appear in any texts at his disposal, certain verses of the Book of Revelation were actually re-translated by Erasmus from Latin into Greek, and that some of these words of Erasmus still hold their place in the Received Text (Textus Receptus), which formed the basis for printed editions of the Greek Testament until the last century.

From the fifteenth century to the present, the equipment with which the New Testament scholar works has been vastly enriched. Discoveries almost as thrilling as the Dead Sea scrolls have given him comparative material with which to work. If some of the manuscripts underlying the Received Text were late, he now has manuscripts like the Codex Sinaiticus, discovered by Constantine Tischendorf at the monastery of St. Catherine at the foot of Mt. Sinai – in a waste paper basket! Competent scholars date this manuscript around A.D. 340. Other ancient texts include the Vaticanus (A.D. 350), the Alexandrinus (A.D. 450), the Ephraem (A.D. 450), the Beza (A.D. 550), the Claromontanus (A.L. 550) and the Washingtoniensis (fourth or fifth century A.D.). The Chester Beatty Papyri, which first came to the attention of scholars in 1931 contain portions of the New Testament, some of which are dated in the third century.

From a careful study of the extant manuscripts of the New Testament, quotations from the Greek Testament in the writings of the Church Fathers, and the versions, or translations made from the Greek into other languages of antiquity, scholars such as Westcott and Hort, Souter, Nestle, and have edited the Greek Testament with the result that our present printed Greek texts are much closer to the original autographs than were the texts used by students of the Greek New Testament a century and more ago.

B. Old Testament.

A parallel development may be noted in Old Testament textual studies. The New Testament has had its "received text," the Old Testament has had its "Masoretic text." In each case it has been recognized that these texts are centuries removed from the originals. In the New Testament field, a succession of discoveries has enabled scholars to reconstruct a text which we have every reason to believe is closer to the original than any one extant text. In the case of the Old Testament, before the Qumran discoveries, we did not have ancient manuscripts. Aside from the Nash Papyrus, a small fragment containing the ten commandments and the Shema (Deuteronomy 6:4), the oldest

Old Testament manuscript, dated A.D. 916, is the Leningrad manuscript of the prophets.

Textual studies in the Old Testament have been hampered by the fact that our manuscripts of the Old Testament are late, and they all reflect a single textual tradition, the so-called Masoretic (i.e. traditional) text. Tradition indicates that, after the fall of Jerusalem, Rabbi Akiba and his associates convened at Jamnia, near the Mediterranean to the west of Jerusalem, to establish the official Hebrew text. It has been alleged that three manuscripts were compared and, in cases of disagreement, the majority of two always determined the "correct" reading. Some scholars think that all texts which did not agree with this accepted text were destroyed. In any case, the second Jewish revolt (A.D. 132-135) which ended in complete victory for the Romans, so reduced the number of Old Testament manuscripts that the official one readily gained supremacy. Professor Frank Cross has noted the fact that the Murabba'at texts agree in a marked way with the Masoretic text. He suggests that the process of fixing an authoritative text was completed in Palestine by the days of the Second Revolt, and concludes that ". . . the movement in biblical interpretation championed by Rabbi Akiba and Aquila stands near the end of the process of establishing an official text – not at the beginning of its struggle for ascendancy."

Professor Paul Kahle, in studying the Isaiah scrolls from Cave 1, Qumran, argued on the basis of differences from the Masoretic text, that the scrolls were hidden in the cave because their text was proscribed, hence not allowed to remain in circulation. The subsequent Qumran finds, representing differing textual traditions, and the archaeological evidence argue against this viewpoint. The process of fixing the text appears to have been completed in the period between the writing of the Qumran texts and the writing of those of Wadi Murabba'at.

II. The Sopherim

The Talmud and the early rabbinical writings describe the work of the *Sopherim,* as the second and third century rabbis were called. In studying the text of Scripture which had been passed on to them, they attempted to fix the pronunciation of certain words and to remove what they deemed superfluous particles from the text. They also indicated by a system of marginal notes certain words which though written, ought not to be read, and others which, though not written, ought to be read. Points were placed above letters or words which were deemed spurious. Scholars do not always agree with their verdict, but the traditions they preserve are useful in discussing textual problems.

III. The Masoretes

The work traditionally associated with Akiba and the *Sopherim* was put into its final form by the Masoretes, whose work ended about the tenth century. They attempted to safeguard the text which had been transmitted to them by "building a hedge" around it. The traditional pronunciation was indicated by a system of vowels and accents. Hebrew, in common with other Semitic languages is written in a consonantal alphabet. To insure the purity of their text the Masoretes counted the verses, words, and even the letters of the books of the Old Testament. They tell how often the same word occurs at the beginning, middle, or end of a verse. They give the middle verse, middle word, and middle letter of each book. The corrections suggested by the *Sopherim* were carefully noted in the margins, but the integrity of the text itself was never tampered with. We owe a great debt to the Masoretes for their care in preserving the traditional Masoretic text for so many centuries.

IV. Ancient Versions

The Old Testament scholar, however, is not able to stop his investigations with the Masoretic text. If he did not, until recently, have ancient manuscripts like the New Testament scholar, he did have other witnesses to pre-Masoretic texts which, in some instances at least, differ from the Masoretic text. The Samaritan Pentateuch, while extant only in late copies, is of pre-Masoretic origin (430 B.C.) and thus represents an independent textual tradition. This is also true of the Greek Septuagint (3rd-2nd centuries B.C.) and the so-called minor Greek versions (early Christian period), although extant texts are of much later date. The Targums, Aramaic paraphrases of the Old Testament, bear witness to the original text, as do Old Testament quotations in the New Testament, the Talmud, and Midrashic literature.

V. Textual Traditions

On the basis of studies in these areas, it has been common knowledge among students of the Old Testament that divergent textual traditions existed. As has been noted, the Masoretic text itself bears witness to this in its marginal notations. Scholarly discussion centered around the nature and extent of such differences, and the validity of considering the Septuagint as a witness to the text of Scripture. It was believed by many able scholars that the Alexandrian translators injected their own theological viewpoints into their translation. The value of the Septuagint was thus confined to the history of interpretation. The value of Septuagint studies in seeking to reconstruct a pre-Masoretic text was denied. While subjective elements must still be considered in evaluating the Septuagint, the Dead Sea Scrolls suggest that its value in textual studies may be greater than previously recognized.

VI. Qumran Biblical Texts

The discovery of ancient Biblical manuscripts in Hebrew (and Aramaic) written before A.D. 70 will certainly revolutionize Old Testament textual studies. Subsequent to the 1947 finds in Cave 1, Qumran, fragments of every Old Testament book except Esther have been identified. Eleven caves have produced ancient manuscripts, at least in fragments, and in some cases many copies of individual books have been identified. Some of these manuscripts represent a textual tradition that appears identical with that which the Masoretes have so carefully preserved for us. Others, we are told, represent a tradition closer to the Septuagint and the Samaritan Pentateuch. Another tradition, differing from all of these is also indicated. It may be noted that the New Testament, when quoting from the Old Testament, sometimes gives a literal rendering of the traditional Hebrew text, sometimes seems to quote from the Septuagint, and sometimes gives a rendering which differs from both.

Although many of the Qumran Biblical texts are not yet available to the student, the information which we now have has caused the whole question of the relationship of the Septuagint to the traditional Masoretic text of the Old Testament to be reopened. Competent scholars have indicated their belief that the Septuagint is a literal translation of a Hebrew text in some respects different from the traditional one. This does not, of course, deny that the Septuagint, like translations in all ages, expresses the theological viewpoint of its translators in many areas, but it does insist that the Septuagint is a witness to an ancient text of the Old Testament as well.

It should be observed that we use the term "different" rather than "better" in discussing the variant textual traditions of the

Old Testament. Since we do not have the original writings of any of the Old Testament books (or, for that matter, of any book of antiquity), the scholar who desires to get as near as possible to the original will compare and contrast the readings provided by his manuscripts and, by the principles of textual criticism, arrive at the text which he deems best after considering all the evidence. In addition to the Masoretic text, the Septuagint, the Samaritan Pentateuch, the Targums, and the ancient versions, the Old Testament student must now consider the evidence of the Qumran texts in studying textual problems.

The extent of changes which may be made in the edited text can be easily exaggerated. While we feel that scholarly modern Greek texts are vast improvements over the old "received text" it should be borne in mind that the difference is not in any sense one of doctrinal import. A scholar of an earlier generation, Bentley, said, "The read text of the sacred writings is competently exact, nor is one article of faith or moral precept either perverted or lost, choose as awkwardly as you will, choose the worst by design out of the whole lump of readings." The arguments put forth by conservatives against modern translations such as the Revised Standard Version seldom bear upon the text behind the version. They usually concern the best translation of words, the meaning of which has been the subject of study and, in some instances, debate, for many years.

VII. Illustrations of Variant Readings

The materials now available for a study of the Old Testament text include the two Isaiah scrolls, the text of the two chapters of Habakkuk in the Habakkuk Commentary, quotations and allusions to Scripture in the sectarian scrolls, and published reports, usually in the form of summary with sample quotations, of some of the finds made subsequent to the discovery of Cave 1. Cave 4 is rich in text material. The Clarendon Press, Oxford, published the first of a projected series of volumes of Cave 4 texts in 1968.

Millar Burrows, in his book *The Dead Sea Scrolls* tells how the Revised Standard Version Committee was able to make use of the St. Mark's Isaiah Scroll (1Q Isa^{a}). Dr. Burrows tells us that thirteen readings in which the manuscript departs from the traditional text were eventually adopted. With pleasing candor he says, "A brief review will show that even in these thirteen places the superiority of the manuscript's reading is not always certain. For myself I must confess that in some places where I probably voted for the emendation I am now convinced that our decision was a mistake, and the Masoretic reading should have been retained." He further tells us that eight of the thirteen readings find some degree of support in the ancient versions.

Illustrations are helpful in showing the type of change which the Dead Sea Scrolls may make in our understanding of the text of Scripture. For example, Isaiah 33:8 contains the words (Revised Standard Version): "Covenants are broken, Witnesses are despised."

The Masoretic text yields a word which is translated "cities" in place of the word which the Revised Stardard Version Committee rendered "witnesses." The difference in Hebrew is in the shape of one letter. The letters "d" and "r" are differentiated only in that the "d" is angular and and the "r" rounded. The same confusion of letters may be noted in the Masoretic text of the Bible where the descendents of Javan in the ethnological list of I Chronicles 1:7 are called "Rodanim," but Genesis 10:4 calls them "Dodanim." Probably both passages refer to the inhabitants of the Island of Rhodes in the Mediterranean.

Isaiah 60:19 is rendered in the Revised Standard Version: "The sun shall be no more your light by day nor for brightness shall the moon give light to you by night."

The Masoretic text omits the words "by night." They occur, however, in the Septuagint, Old Latin, and Aramaic versions, as well as in the St. Mark's scroll.

The addition of an "i" to the Hebrew word translated "marred" in both the Authorized and Revised Standard versions of Isaiah 52:14 yields a word which may be translated, "I anointed" (so Brownlee). "His appearance was so marred" would then be rendered, "I anointed his appearance." This reading has not been accepted in any standard translation, but it has been considered a witness to Qumran Messianic thinking. Joseph Rider objects to this viewpoint accounting for the added letter by "the fondness of the copyist for vowel letters."

Whatever adds to our knowledge of Hebrew vocabulary also adds to our knowledge of the Old Testament. In this sense the sectarian scrolls will play their part in Biblical lexicography. Amos 2:6, speaking of the transgressions of Israel, says: ". . . they sell the righteous for silver and the needy for a pair of shoes."

Although the text makes good sense as translated, it has been pointed out that the word rendered "a pair of shoes" (one word in Hebrew) may also be rendered "a bribe." Suggestions of this type must be carefully weighed, but such light as vocabulary from the sectarian scrolls can throw on the text of Scripture will be welcomed by the serious student. The papyri have added immensely to our understanding of New Testament vocabulary. The scrolls may do the same for the words of the Old Testament.

The basic text of the Hebrew Bible is consonantal. The Masoretes have, as we have seen, developed a system of vocalization in accordance with the traditional interpretation of Scripture. Scholars have felt more free to change the vocalization of the Masoretic text than the consonantal text itself.

Isaiah 49:12 closes with the words: ". . . and these [shall come] from the land of Sinim."

Some have identified the Sinim with the Chinese. The vowels in the St. Mark's Isaiah scroll seem to indicate a reading "the land of Syene" or Yeb, in Upper Egypt.

While details of interpretation may seem inconsequential to many, it should be remembered that the scholar esteems nothing inconsequential which throws light on his subject. To the Old Testament scholar, his prime concern is with the text of Scripture. He does not have the autographs of Moses, or Isaiah, or Ezekiel, or any of the others who were used of God in giving him his Bible. He is thankful for the fact that his Old Testament and his New Testament texts are reliable transcripts of the message of the inspired writers. He recognizes that human fallacy has introduced minor errors and misunderstandings, and seeks to use every means at his disposal to secure a text as free as possible from these errors. The discovery of scrolls by Arab Bedouin near the Wadi Qumran is both a witness to the antiquity of the Biblical text and a tool for its careful study.

9

THE SCROLLS AND THE INTEGRITY OF SCRIPTURE

Opposing viewpoints concerning the message of the scrolls have been uttered by friends and foes of evangelical Christianity. To some, the scrolls prove that Christianity is but a natural development of ideas which had been making the rounds of pre-Christian religious thought. Men like Edmund Wilson and A. Powell Davies are confident that Christianity as we know it will soon be a thing of the past.

On the other hand some evangelical writers have insisted that the inspiration of the Bible is now capable of objective proof. To them the Bible has been "proved" by the Qumran finds, just as dogmatically as to their opposites it has been "disproved."

I. Inspiration

Certain questions which people ask about Scripture cannot be answerel on the basis of archaeological finds. Inspiration, for example, is in the realm of theology and discoveries cannot either "prove" or "disprove" theological postulates of this type.

It is proper and necessary, however, to examine the historical bases of the tenets of theology. Since Christian theology is based on objective reality it cannot be satisfied to remain ignorant of fact from whatever sphere fact may be presented. When an archaeologist finds evidence that Sennacherib besieged the city of Jerusalem in the days of king Hezekiah he does not thereby "prove" the inspiration of Scripture, but he does present evidence that the history contained in the Bible is reliable. Belief in the inspiration of the Bible is thus not incongruous.

While the Dead Sea Scrolls can neither prove nor disprove inspiration, they clearly indicate that a community of Jews more than nineteen centuries ago possessed a library of sacred writings which, in all essential details, is the same as the Bible which we have regarded as authoritative. They also had books which we term apocryphal, as well as works distinctive to their sect. Their regard for the Old Testament was, however, supreme. Commentaries were written on its books. Scholars who have examined the manuscripts assert that the Biblical scrolls are written in a style of writing which is distinctive – as if to mark them off for special consideration. Those who believe in an inspired Bible find much encouragement in the Qumran texts.

II. Canon

The canon is the collection of Biblical books received as genuine and inspired. The Jewish synagogue and the Protestant church have the same canon of the Old Testament. The Roman Catholic church accepts the 39 books of this canon as inspired, but it also accepts the collection of books which are known as apocrypha as part of the Catholic Bible.

We would like to know what books were deemed canonical by the Qumran community. A simple answer cannot be given because of the very nature of ancient writing materials. Each book existed as a single scroll. There is no bound collection of writings – such as our Bible – of which one could say, "These are our sacred books." The leaders of the Qumran community could have told us which of the scrolls were considered inspired Scripture, but no list of such writings has come down to us. In some sense all of the documents kept in the library were considered authoritative – even the commentaries – but as Jews faithful to the tradition of the fathers there was doubtless a special regard for the Law (or Torah). Creeds, confessions of faith, and other writings are considered binding by Christian communities which consider the Bible as the word of God in a unique sense.

Indicative of the fact that the Old Testament as we have it was regarded as sacred Scripture at Qumran is the fact that every book except Esther is represented, at least in the form of fragments. In editing the Zadokite work, Chaim Rabin notes that quotations or allusions to every book in the Old Testament except Joshua, Joel, Jonah, Haggai, Ruth, and Lamentations are made in that document. Since the Zadokite work is related to the Qumran community, and copies of it have been found at

Qumran, this gives added testimony to the canon of Scripture. Thus every book of the Old Testament is found either in manuscript, quotation, or allusion in the Qumran literature. The absence of Esther from the Qumran library may be due to the fact that it was not composed among Palestinian Jews. Since its locale is Persia it may not have been well known by the Qumranians. It is not quoted in the New Testament.

While apocryphal literature is found in abundance among the Qumran documents it is worthy of note that all of the commentaries thus far identified are of canonical books. In addition to the Cave 1 Habakkuk Commentary, fragments have been found of commentaries on Genesis 49, Psalms 37, 45, 57, 68; Isaiah (one in Cave 3 and another in Cave 4), Hosea, Micah, Nahum, and Zephaniah. It would appear that only the canonical books were considered important enough to warrant interpretative commentaries.

III. Criticism

Written centuries after the traditional dates of the writing of the Biblical books (e.g. Isaiah lived in the 8th century B.C., Daniel in the 6th century B.C.) the Biblical scrolls from Qumran are centuries removed from their originals. Thus they do not bear immediate answers to the questions which critics have raised (e.g. Did Isaiah write all of the book attributed to him? Is Daniel a Maccabean pseudepigraphical work?).

Nevertheless they do argue for a much earlier date than some have been willing to admit. Not only do we possess manuscripts from the second century before Christ, but these manuscripts give evidence of a long textual history having preceded them. Divergent texts and families of texts are in themselves eloquent witnesses to the antiquity of their originals. While definite dates cannot be proved by such evidence, the antiquity of the documents discussed cannot be seriously questioned.

The Isaiah scrolls were the first Biblical texts found, and the first to receive serious study. There is no hint in either of these scrolls of a "deutero-" or "trito-Isaiah," to use the language of modern scholarship. The advocate of two or three "Isaiahs" may suggest that the book was put in its present form prior to the writing of the Qumran manuscripts, but the fact remains that our oldest pre-Christian manuscripts bear witness to the text substantially as we have it in our printed Hebrew Bibles.

The Habakkuk Commentary, however, covers only the first two chapters of the canonical book. The blank space on the last

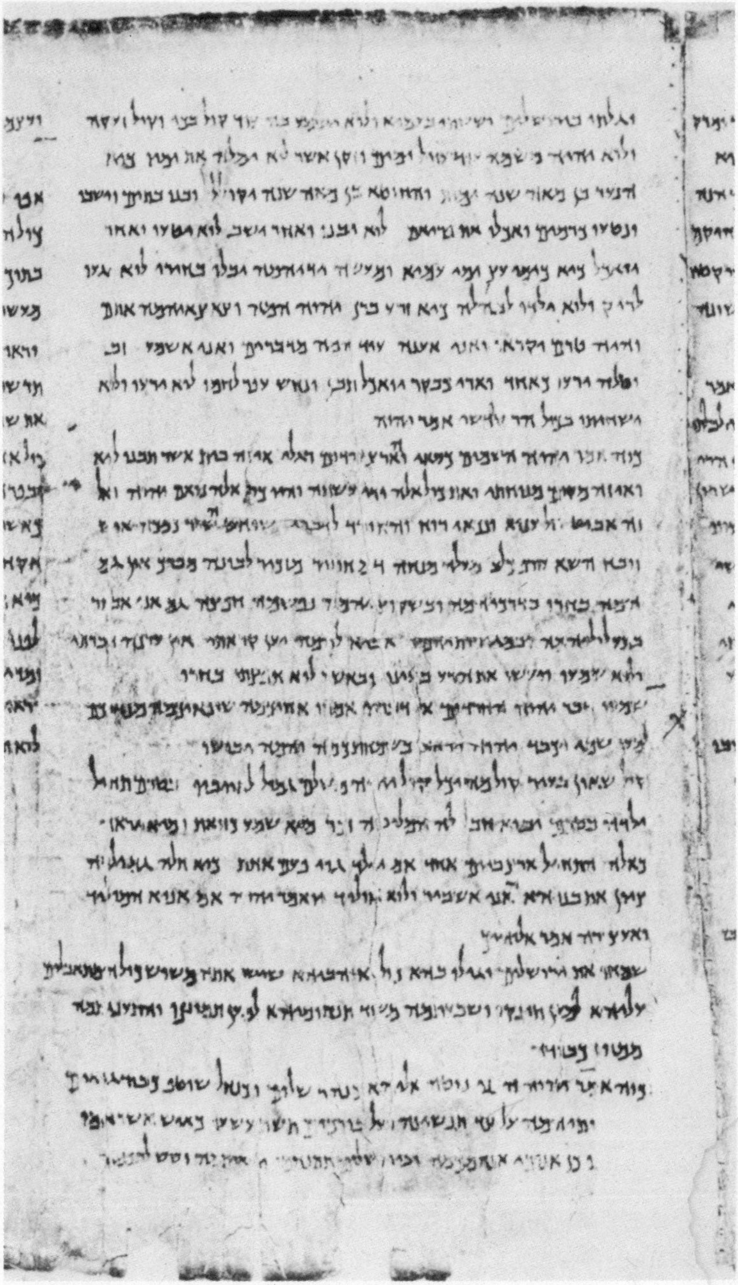

A PAGE FROM THE ISAIAH SCROLL, Cave 1. Courtesy Millar Burrows.

leaf of the commentary is evidence that the commentary ended at that point. The third chapter of Habakkuk is in the form of a psalm written by the prophet. It may not have been the purpose of the commentator to include the psalm in his commentary, for he was expounding those chapters of Habakkuk which he could interpret in the light of the history of his sect. The commentaries frequently discuss portions of books rather than entire books. It is, of course, also possible that the psalm which we now know as the third chapter of Habakkuk circulated separately before being joined to the prophetic portion of Habakkuk's writings to form one book.

The presence of the Book of Daniel at Qumran has been hailed as evidence for the sixth century date of the Biblical book. Accepting A.D. 68 as the last date when manuscripts were copied (assuming that the scrolls were hidden then from the advancing Roman legions) it is unwise to appeal to the scrolls as affording "proof" of the early date of Daniel. Daniel is in the Septuagint and is quoted in the New Testament. Its presence among the scrolls indicates that it was among the books studied at Qumran. Certainly all of the evidence accords with the traditional sixth century date. A Maccabean date would allow little time for its canonization, presence in the Septuagint, the New Testament – and Qumran.

It should be noted that, while negative higher critical views of the Bible cannot be refuted by a study of the Qumran scrolls, there is no evidence from Qumran to justify a major reassment of traditional views of the origin of Biblical writings. The Old Testament books from Qumran are those which we find in our Bibles. Minor textual variants occur as they do in any document which depends on hand copies for multiplication, but the Biblical texts may be regarded as essentially reliable.

10

BIBLICAL INTERPRETATION AT QUMRAN

The Qumran sect, like orthodox Jews and Christians of every generation, had a deep reverence for the Scriptures as the very Word of God. The men of Qumran had separated themselves from the main stream of Jewish life in order to "prepare the way of the Lord" by studying His Law. The Manual of Discipline (6:7) orders that "there shall not cease to be a man who expounds the Law day and night." Life was so arranged in the community center that the men took turns in applying themselves to Bible study on a "round the clock" basis.

The study of the Law had a practical purpose. Scripture was looked upon as a guide to conduct "until the coming of the prophet and the Messiahs of Aaron and Israel" (9:11). The sect thought of itself as the true Israel, and occupied itself with the interpretation of Scripture as it awaited the consummation of history and the vindication of its distinctive teaching.

Although the Sadducees limited their canon to the five books of Moses, the Qumran community had an equally high regard for the Prophets. Whether they, like other Jews, regarded the inspiration of the Prophetic Books as on a lower level than that of the Law (our Pentateuch), we have no way of knowing. In practice, they placed considerable emphasis on the expounding of the Prophetic Books as is evidenced by the many commentaries which have survived.

Much of what went on at the Qumran community has long been forgotten. We do, however, have fragments of quite a number of commentaries which were either produced at Qumran or, at least, studied there. In addition to the Cave 1 Habakkuk Commentary (pages 66-77) we also have fragments of commentaries on Micah and Zephaniah (Cave 1); Hosea and Nahum (Cave 4); Isaiah (Caves 3 and 4); Genesis 49 and Psalms (Caves 1 and 4). Father J. T. Milik and Dr. Frank M. Cross are among the scholars who regard these Qumran documents as the original autographs. Whether or not this is true, the commentaries do illustrate the attitude of the Qumran community toward Scripture and its interpretation.

Milik has noted three aspects of Biblical interpretation which he has observed in the commentaries. (1) Some deal primarily with the life of the sect, interpreting the Biblical prophecies as a prediction of the history of the community and the trials which befell its leaders. The commentaries on Habakkuk, Micah, and Psalms are placed in that category. (2) Other commentaries, Milik notes, apply Scripture to the various ethnic groups which were contemporaneous with the Qumran sect. The Nahum Commentary with its reference to "Demetrius, king of Greece," is cited as an example. (3) Still others are primarily eschatological in tone. The Isaiah 10-11 commentary which speaks of "the latter days to come" is so classified. This attempt to categorize each of the commentaries appears at times to be artificial, for in a large work such as the Habakkuk Commentary all three aspects can be illustrated. Milik has, however, called our attention to elements which we are likely to find in the Qumran commentaries.

Negatively we must state that the Qumran sect was not interpreted in the historical backgrounds of the Old Testament Scriptures or in the immediate context to which the prophetic writings applied. They felt that Scripture was designed to illuminate their own history and that it was relevant to the times in which they lived—which they felt were the end times. Although the Biblical prophets had much to say about nations such as Assyria and Babylon, under whom Israel and Judah were taken into exile, they are never mentioned at Qumran for the simple reason that they were not political states at the time the Qumran commentaries were written.

For this reason we cannot expect the commentaries to throw any light on the meaning of the Old Testament writings themselves. They help us to understand the attitudes of pre-Christian sectarian Judaism, and for this reason they are valuable to the historian and the Biblical scholar who is interested in the backgrounds of the New Testament. Principles of interpretation exhibited in the Qumran Commentaries may be compared with the use of Old Testament Scripture in the New Testament.

I. The Qumran Commentary Made Collections of Old Testament Scripture Portions.

An important Cave 4 document, known as the *Testimonia,* quotes Deuteronomy 5:28-29 and 18:18 together in such a way as to give them a unified meaning without reference to the intervening chapters. The passage thus reads:

> I have heard the words of this people, which they have spoken to you; they have rightly said all that they have spoken. Oh that they had such a mind as this always, to fear me and keep all my commandments, that it might go well with them and with their children for ever. I will raise up for them a prophet like you from among their brethren; and I will put my words in his mouth, and he shall speak to them all that I command him.

The *Testimonia* goes on to quote Numbers 24:15-17, Deuteronomy 33:8-11 and a selection from an apocryphal work known

THE "SCROLLERY" at the Rockefeller Museum, Jerusalem, where an international team of scholars reconstructed and studied pages from the Qumran library. Courtesy, Palestine Archaeological Museum.

as the Psalms of Joshua, other fragments of which were found in the same cave.

A selection of passages from Exodus, II Samuel, Psalms, Isaiah, and Amos, known as the *Florilegium*, contains verses which the Qumran community interpreted as Messianic. The prophecy of Nathan concerning David (II Samuel 7:11-14) is elaborated with a description of a Davidic Messiah who would appear in the last days with a "teacher of the Law."

It is of interest to the New Testament student that the words "I will be his father, and he shall be my son" (II Samuel 7:14), quoted in Hebrews 1:5 as fulfilled in Jesus, are interpreted Messianically in the *Florilegium*. Similarly Amos 9:11, "And I will raise up the booth of David that is fallen," appears both in the *Florilegium* and in the New Testament (Acts 15:16). The *Florilegium* comments, "That is the booth of David that is fallen, but afterward he will arise to save Israel."

The Book of Acts refers to II Samuel 7:12-14 as evidence that God had sworn to David "that he would set one of his descendants upon his throne" (Acts 2:30). James, in seeking to vindicate Peter's mission to the Gentiles quoted Amos 9:11-12 beginning, "I will raise up the booth of David that is fallen."

The discovery of the Qumran *Testimonia* and *Florilegium* renders plausible the suggestion of New Testament scholars that the early church made use of collections of Old Testament quotations which were used in teaching. Old Testament passages which were considered to be Messianic and fulfilled in the Person and ministry of Christ seem to have been brought together into *Testimonia* similar to those at Qumran.

Quotations in Matthew's Gospel frequently are introduced by a formula which reads: "All this took place to fulfil what the Lord had spoken by the prophet . . ." or some variant (cf. 1:22; 2:17, 3:3). These quotations tend to follow the Hebrew text of the Old Testament, whereas Matthew's quotations which are not preceded by such formulae often agree with the Greek Septuagint. J. M. Allegro has suggested that Matthew drew on a pre-Masoretic textual tradition similar to that used by the translators of the Septuagint when not using the "formula" passages. This textual tradition is known from other Qumran writings, notably the Cave 4 Samuel Scroll.

The use of *Testimonia* by New Testament writers may account for composite quotations such as Matthew 21:5:

> Tell the daughter of Zion,
> Behold, your king is coming to you

humble, and mounted on an ass
and on a colt, the foal of an ass.

This appears to be a conflation of Isaiah 62:11

Say to the daughter of Zion,
Behold your salvation comes. . . .

with Zechariah 9:9:

Rejoice greatly, O daughter of Zion!
Shout aloud, O daughter of Jerusalem!
Lo, your king comes to you;
triumphant and victorious is he,
humble and riding on an ass,
on a colt the foal of an ass.

Testimonia were gathered from various parts of Scripture and integrated into virtually new compositions. This may account for the fact that Matthew 27:9 is ascribed to Jeremiah, when actually it is a paraphrase of Zechariah 11:13 with possible overtones from Jeremiah 18:2-3 and 32:6-15. Collections of *Testimonia* probably derived their names from the first author quoted. Matthew, then, would be referring to his direct source, the *Testimonia,* which bore the name of Jeremiah rather than the ultimate source of his quotation, Zechariah's prophecy.

II. The Qumran Community Applied Historical References in Scripture to Contemporary Situations.

The Nahum Commentary comments on the words, "Where the lion went . . ." (Nahum 2:11) and identifies the lion as "Demetrius, king of Greece." Demetrius, we read, "tried to come to Jerusalem by the counsel of the seekers of smooth things." The "seekers of smooth things" were those who, from the viewpoint of the sect, sought an easy life through compromise of their basic Jewish convictions.

The Demetrius of the Nahum Commentary was probably Demetrius III who invaded Judea *ca.* 88 B.C. in the days of Alexander Jannaeus. The Pharisees who were opposed to Jannaeus may be the "seekers after smooth things" who encouraged Demetrius to attack Jerusalem.

Another individual mentioned in the Nahum Commentary is "the lion of wrath" who "took vengeance on the seekers of smooth things in that he proceeded to hang them up alive (which was never done) in Israel before, for concerning one hung up above on (the) tree the Scripture says . . ." This "lion of wrath" is probably Alexander Jannaeus himself, who, according to Josephus, crucified eight hundred Jews who had rebelled against him (Antiquities XIII. 376).

A document known as the *Psalms of Joshua* has been preserved in fragments from Cave 4 and in a quotation in the *Testimonia.* In Milik's reconstruction the extant portions read:

> At the time when Joshua finished praising and giving thanks in his praises, he said: "Cursed be the man who will build this city; with his first born he will lay its foundation and with his last born he will set up its gates. And behold, cursed be the man of Belial who stands forth to be a fowler's snare for his people and destruction to all his neighbors. And he stood forth and made his sons rulers, and both of them became vessels of violence. And they built again this city, and established for it a wall and towers to provide a refuge for wickedness (in the land and a thing of great shame) in Israel, a horrible portent in Ephraim and in Judah . . . and they wrought apostasy in the land and a thing of great shame among the sons of Jacob. And they poured forth blood like water on the ramparts of the daughter of Zion, and in the bounds of Jerusalem."

The writer appears to be applying the words of Joshua originally spoken concerning Jericho, to Jerusalem. An unnamed ruler placed his two sons as rulers of the city and, in the eyes of the author of the *Testimonia,* they became "vessels of violence," words used in Genesis 49:5 of Levi and Simeon. The sons built the city with "a wall and towers" and it became "a refuge for wickedness." The writer of the *Testimonia* heartily disapproves of both the father and his two sons. Identification of the characters is not easy, and no solution has solved all the problems. Milik identifies the sons who rebuilt Jerusalem with Jonathan and Simon whose labors spanned the decade from 152 to 142 B.C. This identification makes the godly priest of Modin, Mattathias, the "man of Belial" of the *Psalms of Joshua.* Milik reminds us, however, that the Qumran community in reacting against the later Hasmonaeans may have overlooked the accomplishments of Mattathias and Judas in leading the revolt against Antiochus Epiphanes and his sympathizers.

III. The Qumran Community Particularized General Biblical Statements.

To the Qumran commentators every word of Scripture has significance without any necessary relationship to its historical context. In Psalm 37:23 we read, "The steps of a man are from the Lord, and he establishes him in whose way he delights." The commentary on Psalm 37 states, "This refers to the priest, the Teacher of [Righteousness]. He has established him to build for him a congregation." Subsequently the commentary quotes Psalm 37:32, "The wicked watches the righteous and seeks to slay him." It then adds, "this refers to the wicked [priest?] who . . . to kill him. . . ." The general statements of Psalm 37 are particularized in the light of the history of the community.

The Habakkuk Commentary comments on the words, "The righteous shall live by his faith" (Habbakuk 2:4) with the observation, "This means all the doers of the Law in the house of Judah, whom God will rescue from the house of judgment because of their labor and their faith in the Teacher of Righteousness." To the Qumran commentators the words of Habakkuk are particularized in such a way as to apply to their own teacher.

IV. The Qumran Community Prepared Paraphrases of Scripture.

Among the Qumran texts we find one example of an extended paraphrase: The Aramaic Midrash of Genesis (mentioned p. 93). Paraphrases from Genesis, Exodus, I and II Samuel have been discovered in Cave 4 along with the *Testimonia* and *Florilegium* which also are paraphrastic in nature.

The Aramaic Midrash of Genesis was edited by Nehum Avigad and Yigael Yadin and published under the title, *A Genesis Apocryphon* by the Magnes Press of the Hebrew University, Jerusalem, in 1956. Although poorly preserved in places, the extant text gives a paraphrase of the Genesis narratives from Noah to Abraham. It serves as an example of the way in which Genesis was interpreted by a segment of pre-Christian Judaism. It may be compared with the more literal Babylonian Targum on the Pentateuch ascribed to Onkelos which was probably written in the third century A.D. on the basis of an earlier paraphrase.

The narrative in the Qumran *Genesis Apocryphon* is given in the first person. After being promised vast lands as an inheritance (Genesis 13:17), Abraham is pictured as going to see the land for himself:

> So I, Abram, went to travel about and see the land. I began to travel from the river Gihon, and I came by the seaside until I reached Ox Mountain; then I traveled from beside this great sea of salt, and went by the side of Ox Mountain to the east, across the breadth of the land until I reached the river Euphrates. I

> traveled along the Euphrates until I reached the Red Sea to the east. I came on beside the Red Sea until I reached the tongue of the Sea of Reeds which goes out from the Red Sea. I traveled to the south until I reached the river Gihon; then I turned back and came to my house in peace, and found all my men well.

The description of Sarah's beauty helps to explain Pharaoh's interest in her, in spite of her advanced age:

> . . . how lovely were her eyes, how delectable her nose, and the whole bloom of her face . . . how lovely her breast, and how beautiful all the whiteness of her; her arms how beautiful, and her hands how perfect, . . . how lovely her palms, and how long and slender each finger of her hands; her feet how beautiful, and how perfect her legs. Of all the virgins and brides that go into the bridal chamber, none is more beautiful than she; yea above all women is she beautiful, and her beauty is high above all of them; yet with all this beauty she has great wisdom. . . .

V. The Qumran Community Possessed Traditions Which Vary from Those of the Canonical Scriptures.

An interesting fragment from Cave 4 contains a prayer ascribed to Nabonidus, known from secular history to have been the father of Belshazzar and the last king of the Neo-Babylonian Empire. Belshazzar served as co-regent with his father who left Babylon and spent seven years at Teima in Arabia. The Qumran fragment states that Nabonidus was smitten with a severe inflamation and was "put far from men." When Nabonidus confessed his sin, God sent to him a prophet who was "a Jew of the exiles in Babylonia." The prophet reminded Nabonidus "that honor should be given, and great glory, to the name of the Most High God." Nabonidus had been afflicted because he prayed "to the gods made of silver and gold, of bronze, of iron, of wood, of stone, of clay."

Scholars have noted the similarity between the history of Nabonidus and the experiences of Nebuchadnezzar described in Daniel 4. Milik suggests that the author of Daniel found the model of his record of Nebuchadnezzar's humiliation in the Prayer of Nabonidus. In Milik's view the unfamiliar name of Nabonidus was changed to Nebuchadnezzar, and the locale of the episode was moved from Teima to Babylon.

Before the discovery of the Prayer of Nabonidus, many scholars observed similarities between the cuneiform records of Nabonidus and the description of Nebuchadnezzar's humiliation. Steinmueller in the *Catholic Biblical Encyclopedia* put forth the view that the ascription of the events of Daniel 4 to Nebuchadnezzar was a copyist's error:

> As the Biblical text in the latter incident (Dan. 4) speaks of the insanity of the king (Dan. 4:28-30) and the cuneiform (inscriptions) inform us that Nabunaid the father of Baltassar (i.e., Belshazzar) suffered from this affliction, it is most likely that a copyist substituted the well-known name Nabuchodonosor (i.e., Nebuchadnezzar) for the lesser known Nabunaid or Nabonidus. (*Catholic Biblical Encyclopedia,* p. 753)

The plausibility of the suggestion that Daniel 4 actually describes an event in the life of Nabonidus is strengthened by the consideration that it does no violence to the chronology of Daniel. Nabonidus chronologically fits between Nebuchadnezzar and Belshazzar (Daniel 5), although Nabonidus was not Nebuchadnezzar's immediate successor.

It is possible, of course, that both Nebuchadnezzar and Nabonidus were judged by God because of their pride and idolatry, and that the Book of Daniel reflects one such judgment and the Prayer of Nabonidus another. There does not appear to be a direct literary relationship between the two works. If they refer to the same event they are independent presentations of the same factual material which entered Jewish tradition in different forms.

VI. The Qumran Community Interpreted Scripture in the Light of Their Eschatological Viewpoint.

The Qumran Community firmly believed that they were living in the end time. Scripture, from their viewpoint, was primarily eschatological in its thrust, and they attempted to identify the details of their prophetic teaching in the Bible. When Psalm 37:10 says, "Yet a little while and the wicked shall be no more," the commentator adds, "This refers to all the wickedness at the end of forty years: when they are finished there will not be found in the land any wicked man."

Within forty years of the death of the Teacher of Righteousness, the Qumran community expected the end of the present order, the punishment of the wicked and the vindication of the righteous. The *Zadokite Work* (see pages 41-42) states that God raised up a true teacher to guide His people "in the way of His heart and to make known to the last generations what He is to do in the last generation against the congregation of the faithless" (1:10-15). The Qumran Community felt itself a part of the "last generations" and they anticipated the "last generation," evidently a forty year period. The eschatological war described in the *War Scroll* (see pages 77-84) was of forty years duration. The end of the war (2:6-10) marked a victory for the "sons of light" over the "sons of darkness."

The Qumran commentators were convinced that God had revealed the mysteries of the latter days in the prophetic writings of Scripture. They also looked upon their Teacher of Righteousness as one raised up of God to give a correct interpretation of the prophetic predictions. The Balaam prophecy, "a star shall come forth out of Jacob, and a scepter shall rise out of Israel" (Numbers 24:17) is interpreted in the *Zadokite Work* as a reference to two eschatological personages: "the star is he who searches the Law. . . . The scepter is the prince of the whole congregation . . ." (5:19-20).

The Cave 4 fragments of a commentary of Isaiah 10 and 11 mention the expectation of a Davidic Messiah whose "sword will execute judgment on all the peoples." A fragment of a commentary on Genesis 49:10 from the same cave is quite explicit:

> For the staff is the covenant of kingship; the thousands of Israel are the feet, until the coming of the Messiah of righteousness, the branch of David, for to him and to his seed is given the covenant of the kingship of his people until eternal generations.

The *Florilegium* said of the Davidic Messiah, "He is the branch of David who will arise with the interpreter of the Law." Although there is no positive evidence that the Qumran community had the concept of a suffering Messiah, it is clear that the Davidic Messiah was not regarded as the sole eschatological figure. Traditionally the political and religious leadership of Israel had been vested in different persons: Moses and Aaron; Solomon and Zadok; Zerubbabel and Jeshua. The Qumran community anticipated a future situation in which there would be "an anointed one from Aaron," i.e., a priestly Messiah, "and from Israel," i.e., a lay or David Messiah (*Manual of Discipline* 9:10-11).

Three eschatological figures: a prophet, an anointed one or Messiah of Aaron, and a Messiah of Israel appear in the Qumran texts. The relation between the prophet and the two "messiahs" is not always clear. Frank M. Cross suggests that in the thinking of the Qumran sect, the Teacher of Righteousness may return as the priestly Messiah. There are Jewish traditions that righteous men of the past will come back to earth during the Messianic Age. A Talmudic Baraita says:

> In the age to come, the son of David (i.e., the Messiah) will be in the middle with Adam, Seth, and Methuselah on his right, and Abraham, Moses, and Jacob on his left.

The presence of Moses and Elijah at the Mount of Transfiguration (Matthew 17:3) illustrates this hope in a Christian context. A comparable hope was expressed by the mother of Zebedee's sons in her request of Jesus:

> Command that these two sons of mine may sit, one at your right hand and one at your left, in your kingdom (Matthew 20:21).

The early church took seriously the ideas of a royal and a priestly Messiah, but insisted that they were the same individual. The Gospels trace the genealogy of Jesus through David and make it clear that his is a royal Messiahship. The Epistle to the Hebrews, moreover, seeks to show that Jesus is also a priestly Messiah, not after the Aaronic order as the Qumran community expected, but after the older and more honorable order of Melchizedek (Hebrews 7). The church likewise ascribes to Jesus the office of prophet. The Qumran expectation of an eschatological prophet, a Messiah of Aaron and a Messiah of Israel finds, in Christian teaching, a perfect fulfillment. All of these functions, indeed all of the promises of God, find expression in the historical Jesus who, in His own person, serves as the perfect Prophet, Priest, and King.

11

QUMRAN MESSIANISM

I. The Word Messiah

The concept of "Messiah" is, of course, much wider than the word. The word, however, has played a particularly important part in the development of the concept. This is true both of the Hebrew *mashiach* and the Greek *Christos,* the latter having served as a title and, in later development, almost a name for Jesus – strictly speaking, *Jeshuah ham-mashiach* ("Jesus the Messiah").

The Hebrew verb *mashach* is thought to have originally borne the significance "to smear, to wipe, or to stroke with the hand." In Biblical usage it is sometimes used in describing secular pursuits. Thus Jeremiah (22:14) speaks of painting a house, i.e., applying color to it. Shields were commonly anointed, or smeared with oil (Isaiah 21:5; II Samuel 1:21).

The anointing with oil was a matter of physical comfort in the warm climate of Bible lands. Hosts frequently used costly unguents as a mark of hospitality toward their guests (cf. Luke 7:46). Women of the wealthy classes anointed their bodies with costly ointments (Amos 6:6, Esther 2:12).

Anointing, however, early was regarded as a suitable religious rite. Jacob poured oil over the stone upon which he had rested his head during his dream of the heavenly ladder (Genesis 28: (Exodus 30:26-29; 40:9-11; Leviticus 8:11). Moses, reckoned as the mediator of the covenant at Sinai, anointed Aaron and his sons for the priestly office (Exodus 28:41; 30:30; Leviticus 8:12). Special anointing oil was prepared for this purpose, making use of olive oil, myrrh, cinnamon, fragrant cane, and cassia (Exodus 30:22-33). It seems legitimate inference that all of the High Priests of the Old Testament were solemnly set aside during a consecration ceremony in which they were anointed with oil.

Kings also were anointed. The High Priest, or a prophet (e.g., Samuel), poured oil from a horned vial upon the head of the king who was thereafter regarded as the "anointed of Yahweh" – the *mashiach Yahweh.*

Although the prophets were charismatic leaders, we know that there were occasions when they, too, were anointed. Before Elijah completed his lightning career he anointed Elisha to serve as his successor (I Kings 19:16).

The term *mashiach,* or "Messiah," as used in post-exilic Judaism and in the Christian church has primary reference to one or more eschatological figures who are the means whereby God delivers His people from their foes and establishes the divine kingdom on earth. The New Testament Messiah, or Christ, was a "son of David" who rightfully came to rule His people and usher in the end of the age, the Messianic era.

The hope of such a Messiah can be traced throughout the Old Testament itself. After the division of the empire of Solomon, the southern kingdom alone remained true to the line of David (II Kings 17:18). Threatened by enemies without (Assyrians, Babylonians), and by spiritual decadence within (cf. Isaiah 1), the pious of Judah looked to God in faith for a deliverer, a righteous scion of David's line who would reign in justice and deliver Israel from her external foes. Jeremiah pictured a day in which Yahweh would write a new covenant on the hearts of his people (Jeremiah 32:31-34). Isaiah saw a "servant of Yahweh" who would suffer (52:13–53:12) and thereby point the way to a true "seed of Abraham" with a message to all the world. Although these passages may not strictly speaking be Messianic, they show something of the hopeful expectancy – as well as the serious heart-searching – of Israel as it contemplated things to come. Neither the Old Testament nor subsequent Jewish theology presented a unified concept of Messiah. Sometimes the word simply means an anointed one." As time went on, however, more and more emphasis was placed on a Messiah or Messiahs who would deliver Israel in its time of need.

II. Messianic Expectation

The two pre-Christian centuries were marked by considerable Messianic ferment. Jewish apocalyptic literature was heralding the impending intervention of God into the historical processes. Daniel had interpreted the seventy years of exile as a foreshadowing of seventy "sevens" – or four hundred ninety years before the establishment of the Messianic kingdom (Daniel 9:24-27). Josephus says of him, "Daniel did not only prophesy of future events as did the other prophets, but he also determined the time of their accomplishment (*Antiquities* X, xi. 7).

The usual date given for the return from the exile is 536 B.C. An interval of 490 years would be ended at 46 B.C. If seventy years are subtracted from 586 B.C., leaving 516 B.C. as the date of the return, Daniel's computations would bring us to 26 B.C.

The New Testament itself gives evidence of this Messianic expectation. Wise men were watching the stars of the East. Simeon was convinced that he would not die before seeing the promised Messiah (Luke 2:26). John the Baptist identified himself – as did the Qumranians – as a voice in the wilderness preparing the way of the Lord. Jesus Himself asserted that the Kingdom of Heaven was at hand.

III. The Teacher of Righteousness

The early history of the Qumran Community is shrouded in mystery. It appears that a group of Hasidim (the "pious") in reaction against the growing Hellenistic influence in Palestine separated themselves from the main body of Judaism. According to the Damascus Zadokite documents they migrated to Damascus and formed a kind of monastic group there. The founder, or at least an important leader of the group was known as the Teacher of Righteousness, or the Righteous Teacher. This leader suffered martyrdom at the hands of "the wicked priest."

Many of the members of this group of Damascus Covenanters turned back from their earlier determination to live as members of the "New Covenant." The Damascus Document condemns them:

> So are all the men who entered into the New Covenant in the land of Damascus, and yet turned backward and acted treacherously, and departed from the spring of living waters. They shall not be reckoned in the assembly of the people, and in its register they shall not be written from the day when there was gathered in the Unique Teacher (i.e., the Teacher of Righteousness) until there shall arise the Messiah from Aaron and Israel (IX:10-29).

This passage is significant in delineating a time span – from the death of the Teacher of Righteousness until the appearance of Messiah. This is the period when the community of the New Covenant is a meaningful entity, existing as the "true Israel" in the wilderness and engaged in the significant ministry of preparing the Way of the Lord.

Concerning the enemy, the Damascus Document notes: ". . . during the period of the destruction of the land there arose those who removed the landmark and led Israel astray. And the land became desolate because they spoke rebellion against the commandments of God through Moses and also through His holy Messiah, and they prophecied a lie to turn Israel away from God" (VII:1-11).

Here the term "Messiah" seems to refer to a historical personage. The implication is that certain commandments were given through Moses and a subsequent "Messiah" – or "anointed one." Although the term could apply to many individuals, the regard of the sect for the Teacher of Righteousness raises the suspicion that he is the "Messiah" here meant. The Habakkuk Commentary from Qumran identifies the "just" who "live by faith" as "those who have faith in the Teacher of Righteousness." Although he is not specifically identified as a Messiah, he does have certain Messianic traits ascribed to him.

A further reference in Damascus Document B contrasts the state of the wicked with that of the righteous:

> And they that give heed unto Him are the poor of the flock! These shall escape during the period of the visitation, but the rest shall be handed over to the sword when the Messiah comes from Aaron and Israel" (B. IX. 10).

A further Damascus Document reference tells of the future ministry of the Messiah:

> Through His Messiah he shall make them (i.e. the righteous) know His Holy Spirit; and He is true, and in the explanation of His name are their names (A. II. 9-10).

One of the interesting puzzles before us is the relation, if any, of the Messiah to the Teacher of Righteousness. Certainly the martyrdom of the Teacher of Righteousness left a profound mark on the community. Was he a Messianic figure?

The remembrance of the career of the Teacher of Righteousness doubtless helped the Hasidic community to shape its

Messianic doctrine. The concept of the suffering Just One had a vivid illustration in the Teacher of Righteousness.

Schonfeld suggests that the Damascus Covenanters believed in two teachers – the historical Teacher of Righteousness who died some time during the middle of the second century B.C., and a second Teacher of Righteousness who may be identified with the Messiah. This second Teacher was a kind of reflection and fulfillment of the almost legendary life and death of the original teacher. Schonfeld goes so far as to suggest that this second Messianic figure may have been regarded as having come in some unspecified person alluded to in the Habakkuk Commentary and the interpolations of the Damascus Document.

Some scholars have suggested that the martyred Teacher of Righteousness was himself expected to return at the end of days as a Messianic figure. There is no specific evidence for this, but it is clear that a Messianic Teacher of Righteousness was expected as the one to usher in the end time and to vindicate the true Israel in its controversy with the enemy.

Did the Damascus Covenanters, and their successors, the Qumran Covenanters, believe in but one Messiah – a kind of reincarnated Teacher of Righteousness? The evidence seems to indicate otherwise.

IV. How Many Messiahs?

Three times the Damascus Document speaks of "the Messiah of Aaron and Israel" (XII. 23; XIV. 19; XIX. 10). The Manual of Discipline, however speaks of "the coming of a Prophet and the anointed ones (*meshiche*)of Aaron and Israel" (1 QS IX. 10-11). The Damascus Document seems to speak of but one Messianic figure, and the Manual of Discipline, three.

Before looking at the Qumran evidence it may be well to glance at other Jewish sources which date to approximately the beginning of the Christian era. The Midrash (Tehill XLIII. 6) is admittedly post-Christian but it appears to embody an old tradition. It reads:

> To that generation [in Egypt] thou didst send redemption through two redeemers, as it is said (Ps. 105:26), 'He sent Moses, his servant, and Aaron whom he had chosen.' And also to this generation [in the Messianic age] he sendeth two, corresponding to the other two: 'Send out thy light and thy truth' (Ps. 43:3). 'Thy light,' that is, the prophet Elijah of the house of Aaron, of whom it is written (Num. 8:2), 'the seven lamps shall throw their light in front of the lampstand.' And 'thy truth,'

> that is Messiah ben David as it is said (Ps. 132:11), 'The Lord hath sworn unto David (in) truth, he will not turn from it.' And likewise it is said (Isa. 42:1), 'Behold thy servant whom I uphold.'

Another Midrash (Num. R. 14) speaks of four eschatological figures: Elijah, the Messiah of Manasseh, the Messiah of Ephraim (The Anointed of War) and the Great Redeemer of the Line of David.

From where did this concept of two (or more) Messiahs come? We have noted that priests, kings, and (sometimes) prophets might be regarded as "anointed ones," and we must be careful lest the term *meshiach* always be interpreted in the sense of an eschatological figure. Still the existence of more than one eschatological figure seems evident from the texts.

Throughout the history of Israel, political and religious interests were frequently in conflict. Saul and Samuel clashed over such a conflict of interests. This became increasingly prevalent with the breakdown of the pre-exilic state. In a sense the captivities came because the political leaders rejected the counsel of those whom we, at least, reckon as prophets.

The return from Babylon had its secular and its religious leaders in close harmony with one another. Zerubbabel and Jeshuah represented, respectively, the civil and religious interests of the Jews. Similarly the great heroes Nehemiah and Ezra represent government and priesthood. There was no presumed conflict between the two, but there was a recognition of the role each played in the life of the nation.

In the fourth chapter of his prophecy, Zechariah depicts two "olive branches" beside two "golden pipes" which empty from themselves oil. By way of identification, Zechariah says, "These are the two sons of clear oil, that stand by the Lord of the whole earth" (4:14). He seems to have in mind the Aaronic priest and the Davidic Prince (Zerubbabel), both of whom are anointed with oil.

The Talmud R. Dosa (A.D. 250) mentions the tradition of two Messiahs: Messiah ben Joseph and Messiah ben David. Messiah ben Joseph was destined to fall in battle against the enemies of Israel. He was killed by the agents of Belial, later identified as Armilus (Romulus, Rome).

The occasion for the name "ben Joseph" has been debated. Some suggest that he is an Ephraimite Messiah, i.e., one from the "Joseph" tribes. Others see in the name a borrowing from Christianity where the father of Jesus is named Joseph. There are older traditions, embodied in a late form in the Testament of Benjamin, iii, of the patriarch Joseph as a type of the righteous man killed by the godless. The Testament of Simeon reads:

> And now my children, obey Levi and Judah, and be not lifted up against these two tribes, for from them shall arise unto you the salvation of God. For the Lord shall raise up from Levi as it were an High Priest, and from Judah, as it were, a king: He shall save all the race of Israel (Sim. vii. 1-2).

The concept of two Messiahs existed in Israel as late as the Second Revolt (A.D. 132-135). One of the coins which date to Bar Kochba mentions: "El'azar the High Priest" and "Shim' on Bar Kochebah, Prince."

The concept of the Davidic Messiah was associated with the victory of God and His people over their mutual foes. The Qumran War Scroll thinks of the ultimate victory of God's people in terms of warfare – a series of eschatological battles, the last of which ushers in the eschaton.

Chaim Rabin in his *Qumran Studies* mentions an interesting parallel in Moslem theology:

> The generic Muslim name for Messianic events is *milhamah*, "war," but in Rabbinic parlance these events are called *hevle hammashiach*, "birth pangs of the Messiah," and the only place, to my knowledge, where *milhamah* occurs in this sense is in a report about the finding of an old Messianic scroll, B.T. San. 97b. In DSW the word occurs in the Messianic sense in the title and again in the "epochs of the wars in Thine hands" (xi. 8). While the Messianic wars in Rabbinic eschatology are fought out by heathen nations, the war of DSW is fought by Israel, begins in the "desert of Jerusalem," and ends forty years later with the conquest of Ham and Japheth. The Muslim *malhama* begins at Medina and ends with the destruction of "Rome" (Constantinople), according to one version by 70,000 "sons of Isaac." Probably the final event of the sectarian war also was the conquest of Rome (p. 118-119).

The Messiah as a "man of war" was complemented by the priestly Messiah. To the Essenes, the Priestly Messiah took precedence over the Royal Messiah. This is particularly borne out in the *Serek ha-edah*, the "order of the congregation," which depicts the communal meal of the eschatological Israel. The order is presented:

> No one [is allowed to touch] the first part of the bread or [of the wine] before the priest. For [he] blesses the first part of the bread and of the wine [and touches] the bread before them. And thereafter shall the Messiah of Israel reach for the bread, [and then only shall the whole congregation say the benedi] ction e[ach according to] his rank (1QSa ii. 18 ff.)

The Messiah of Israel here stands second in rank to "the priest," a reference to the presiding priest, or High Priest. This priest must be the "Messiah of Aaron" mentioned in the formula "the Messiahs of Aaron and Israel."

The section of the *Serek ha-edah* which immediately precedes that quoted above illustrates the strict concept of order and rank within the Qumran Community:

> [And the Priest], the Anointed One, shall come with them, [for he is] the head of the entire Congregation of Israel; [and before him shall sit the sons] of Aaron, the priests; and the [conveners] of the assembly [?], the honored men, they shall sit [before him, each] according to his place of rank. And then [shall come the Messi]ah of Israel; and before him shall sit the heads [of the tribes, each] according to his place of honor, according to [their . . .] in their "camps" and their march formations; and all heads [of the houses of the Congregat]ion together with the wi[se men of Israel] shall sit before them, each according to his proper place of rank (I QSa ii. 12-17).

V. Conclusions

The Qumran *Serek* speaks of three eschatological figures: a prophet, Messiah of Aaron, and Messiah of Israel. It is conceivable that the group at one time looked for but one Messianic figure, as indicated in the Damascus Documents, but by the time the Serek was composed a plurality existed. There is no clear relationship between the Teacher of Righteousness and these eschatological personages, although there is evidence of an eschatological Teacher of Righteousness. F. L. Cross and Stendahl suggest that the Teacher of Righteousness will return and accompany the Messianic figures. There are traditions that Abraham, Moses, and other righteous men of past ages will do likewise – an idea which finds a parallel in the Gospel account of the transfiguration of Jesus.

The early church took seriously the ideas of a priestly and a royal Messiah as held at Qumran and elsewhere in the Jewish community. The Gospels trace the genealogy to David and make it clear that His is a royal Messiahship. The Epistle to the

Hebrews, however, seeks to show that Jesus is also a Priestly Messiah, not after the Aaronic order but after that of Melchizedek which is older and more honorable than that of Aaron. The church likewise sees in Jesus the office of the prophet. The historic designation of Jesus as "prophet, priest, and king" finds an almost perfect parallel at Qumran with its eschatological prophet, Messiah of Aaron, and Messiah of Israel.

12

GNOSTICISM AND THE QUMRAN LITERATURE

Gnosticism is one of those movements which defy definition. As known in the second and third centuries of the Christian era it consisted of a fusion of different and previously independent beliefs and customs. The Hellenistic age was one of syncretism. The Greek Zeus became Zeus-Amon-Re in Egypt and Zeus-Baal-Shamayim in Syria. The gods of Greece and Rome were identified, and cult practices from the far reaches of the Empire were adopted or adapted.

Properly speaking, Gnosticism may not be identified before the second Christian century, and the time of its zenith was the third and fourth centuries. Its antecedents, however, may be traced back to the most remote antiquity. Egypt, Mesopotamia, and even India produced elements which appear in Gnostic thought. The Gnostic pictured the spirit of man, stripped of all foreign accretions, finally reaching God, an idea which is comparable to the Hindu doctrine of Nirvana.

Greek mythology and philosophy and the Hebrew-Christian Scriptures, with the body of apocryphal and pseudepigraphical literature which developed immediately before and after the time of Christ, form the more immediate background for Gnostic thought. The Qumran literature is contemporaneous with this latter period.

The Jewish-Christian literature of the Hellenistic age is, itself, the product of the tendency toward syncretism. The Essenes, usually identified as the group responsible for the Qumran literature, although professedly the most orthodox of Jewish groups, adopted customs related to Egyptian and Persian thought. The custom of turning the face toward the sun in prayer is not of Biblical origin. It appears to reflect usage traceable to Egypt.

On the other hand, certain forms of Gnositicism reacted against the Old Testament, identifying the God of the Old Testament with the Demiurge – an inferior deity who was responsible for the creation of matter. Marcion's canon of Scripture purposely eliminated all references to Judaism and the God of the Old Testament.

The Qumran literature cannot, of course, be expected to yield the full-orbed Gnosticism of the third century. The most we can find at Qumran is the existence of certain tendencies which, together with other tendencies from other sources, became the familiar Gnosticism of Valentinus, Basilides, and their school.

I. Dualism

Although not limited to the Gnostics, dualism was an important element in Gnostic thought. Thinking people of many cultures have been puzzled about the relationship between the spiritual and the material, the good and the bad. Cosmological dualism deals with the relationship between spirit and matter. The concepts of the good and the bad are the province of ethical dualism. The areas may be related, as they are in Gnosticism when the evil is equated with the material and the good with the spiritual. This equation is not necessary, however.

The equation of the evil with the material raises important problems. How can God, who is spirit and good, create a world which is material, hence bad? The Gnostics tried to meet this problem by positing a series of emanations from the divine Spirit. These emanations bring into being the Demiurge who is responsible for the creation of the material universe. Thus the Gnostics have removed the universe, as far as their system would allow, from God.

The Gnostic who considered himself Christian had the further problem in accounting for the incarnation and the resurrection. How could the divine, sinless Christ dwell in a material, hence evil, body? An answer came in the form of docetism – Christ did not really have a human body. He "seemed" to dwell in a body of flesh and blood, but this was only appearance. Orthodoxy quite properly resisted the docetic teaching, and insisted on the true humanity as well as the true deity of Christ.

Dualism is frequently traced to Persian Zoroastrianism. Mani, who tried to synthesize Zoroastrianism with Buddhism and Christianity, declared, "Two beings were at the beginning of the world: the one, light; the other, darkness." This self-conscious dualism which Persian religion developed made an impact on the Greco-Roman world, but it must not be considered native to Persia. The motif of the conflict between good and evil appears in the Babylonian creation epic, the *Enuma Elish,* in which Marduk overcomes the monster *Tiamat,* and from her divided body makes heaven and earth. Although there is certainly no historical relationship, this may be compared with the Gnostic concept of Achamoth, the formless creature of Sophia, who was given form and became the basic element of the universe.

The ethical type of dualism is common to John's Gospel and Epistles, the *Didaché,* and the Qumran *Serek* and War Scroll. Many New Testament scholars now regard the Johannine literature as a reflection of pre-Christian Jewish thought, rather than post-Christian Greek concepts. This is not a denial of Greek influence, but a pushing-back of that influence to the earlier period. Lucetta Mowry, writing in the *Biblical Archaeologist,* observes, "It seems likely that John wrote under the impact of an ethical dualism found in the Essene documents, and that his system finds its appropriate place as we set his gospel beside them.

The *Didaché* begins with a six chapter discussion of "The Two Ways." According to Robert M. Grant, these chapters are "undoubtedly derived from Jewish or Christianized Jewish tradition." Although orthodox, rather than Gnostic (regarded, however as Montanist by some scholars) the beginning of the Didaché illustrates the concept of ethical dualism which found repeated expression in the Hellenistic-Roman age, "There are two ways, one of life, and one of death, and between these two ways there is a great difference." The Qumran *Serek* requires those who "enter the covenant" to "love all the sons of light" and "hate all the sons of darkness." After discussing the two spirits, the Spirit of Truth and the Spirit of Perversity, the *Serek* states, "Between these two categories He has set eternal enmity." We are assured, however, of the ultimate victory of the "Spirit of Truth" for "Perversity shall be no more, and all works of deceit shall be put to shame."

The Qumran *War Scroll,* as previously noted on pages 77-84, describes a series of battles known as "the war of the sons of light with the sons of darkness." The "sons of darkness" are powerful and win battles, but the outcome of the war is assured. The "sons of light" win the ultimate victory.

While recognizing the presence of evil, the Qumran documents nowhere attempt a philosophical, or even a theological account of its origin. The *Serek* says, "The origin of truth lies in the Fountain of Light, and that of perversity in the Well-spring of Darkness" (3:19).

This Qumran, Jewish dualism did not follow Persian Dualism in assuming the eternal existence of two opposing forces. Without concern for the moral problems involved, the Qumranians boldly stated, "It is God that created these spirits of light and darkness, and made them the basis of every act, the instigators of every deed, and the directors of every thought" (3: 25-26). Thus a rigid monotheism is preserved. The world may be classified as evil and good, but God is the author of both. As in the parables of Jesus, evil is permitted until the final judgment, when right alone will prevail and persist.

Josephus said of the Essenes, with whom the Qumran community appears to be related, "These Essenes reject pleasures as an evil, but esteem continence, and the conquest over our passions, to be virtue. They neglect wedlock, but choose out other persons' children, while they are pliable, and fit for learning; and esteem them to be of their kindred, and form them according to their own manners" (II, viii, 2-14). All of the Essenes did not enforce celibacy, and there is evidence from the cemetery adjoining the Qumran community center that women were buried there. Nevertheless the tendency of Essene life was clearly in the direction of asceticism. The ascetic is apt to regard the physical side of life as sinful, or, at least, as on a lower plane than that which he esteems as spiritual. Asceticism was in no sense limited to the Gnostics, and the celibacy of the Roman Catholic priesthood indicates its hold on traditional Catholicism, but it appears to be an outgrowth of a dualistic viewpoint. It would have seemed utterly fantastic to Abraham to have been told that celibacy was a state to be preferred to matrimony.

The Essene doctrine of immortality shows clear traces of cosmological dualism: "For their doctrine is this: That bodies are corruptible, and that the matter they are made of is not permanent; but that the souls are immortal, and continue for ever; and that they come out of the most subtle air, and are united to their bodies as in prisons, into which they are drawn by a certain natural enticement; but that when they are set free from the bonds of the flesh, they then, as released from a long bondage, rejoice and mount upward" (Josephus). Josephus admits that this view is similar to that of the Greeks. From the concept of dualism, there develops a doctrine of deliverance from the flesh, a "salvation" which liberates the soul from his prison house and enables him to return to the "most subtle air" which is the proper abode of the non-material part of man. As we shall observe, this idea is adopted by the Gnostics and becomes an integral part of their system.

When Gnosticism developed in the second and third centuries, dualism was a common phenomenon. It had existed in embryo from the most remote history of the Near East. It gained momentum in Zoroastrian Persia. Jews at Qumran used its concepts within the framework of monotheism. The writings of John likewise spoke of "darkness" and "light" as the ethical forces which the Christian must meet (Cf. John 1:5; 3:19; 12:35; I John 1:5; 2:8). Paul spoke of the flesh lusting against the spirit (Galatians 5:17). Against such a background the dualism of Gnosticism must be traced.

II. Esoteric Knowledge

The idea of knowledge is inherent in the very word Gnosticism. The *gnosis,* however, is hidden and esoteric, known only to the initiates. By this special knowledge man may become spiritual and, therefore, good, according to Gnostic ideas. The soul is thought of as liberating itself progressively from its imprisonment in matter by ascending through the spheres to the upper realm of spirit. Revealed *gnosis,* knowledge, or the use of a name, or a potent formula, accomplished this liberation for the initiate.

The *gnosis* of which the Gnostic speaks must be thought of in terms of intellectualism. The Gnostics did frequently attempt to make Christianity palatable to the intellectuals of their time, but their method was not that of modern intellectualism. Gnosis was revealed, not attained by the unaided intellect.

It is clear that this idea is not foreign to that of Scripture, with its doctrine of revelation and regeneration. Scripture knows nothing of the praxis of later Gnosticism, but it does stress the existence of a knowledge which "none of the princes of this world knew: for had they known it, they would not have crucified the Lord of glory" (I Corinthians 2:8). To the Christian, Christ is the One "In whom are hid all the treasures of wisdom and knowledge" (Colossians 2:3).

Qumran literature has much to say about knowledge, but its references are more akin to Scriptural ideas than to those of later Gnosticism. God is spoken of as "the God of knowledge"

(*Manual of Discipline* 3:15) and "the source of knowledge" (10:12). It is "by His knowledge" that "everything has been brought into being" (11:11).

In the person of the Teacher of Righteousness we meet certain ideas which savor of Gnosticism. The Habakkuk Commentary describes him as one "to whom God has made known all the mysteries of the words of His servants, the prophets" (7:5). He seems to have been considered an infallible interpreter of Scripture, and the sect which treasured his interpretations had a kind of *gnosis*.

The Qumran vocabulary includes several words which seem to have an esoteric connotation. Such a word is *sod*, "secret" or "counsel," which occurs in a context in which the supervisor is required to be "master of every secret of men" *Zadokite Documents*, 14:9-10). Of frequent occurrence is the word *razim*, "mysteries," which occurs nine times in the Aramaic sections of the canonical Book of Daniel. The Septuagint renders the word *razim* as *musterion*.

Other words which are of significance in a discussion of Gnosticism are *satar*, particularly in the form *nistarot*, "hidden things," *bîn*, "understanding," and *sekel*, "insight."

A common Gnostic idea is that the soul, on leaving the body, finds its path to the highest heaven opposed by the deities and demons of the lower realms of heaven. Only when in possession of the names of the demons, or a formula for their exorcism, can the individual make his way to his proper heavenly home. The knowledge of the names of the demons has been regarded by some as the central doctrine of Gnosticism.

The Bible itself names but two angels, Gabriel and Michael. The apocryphal and pseudepigraphical literature developed a complex angelology which was adopted in some circles of Jewish and, later, Christian thought. In describing the solemn oaths taken by members of the Essene sect, Josephus notes, ". . . he swears to communicate their doctrines to no one any otherwise than as he received them himself; that he will abstain from robbery, and will equally preserve the books belonging to their sect, and the names of the angels. These are the oaths by which they secure their proselytes to themselves" (II, viii, 2-14).

This solitary reference to "the names of the angels" does not tell us much about Essene angelology. It is even possible that the "angels" are simply human messengers. The word *angelos* can bear that meaning. In the Qumran literature, however, the spirits of light and darkness which struggle in man's soul, and in the universe, are sometimes called angels. The elect are described as sharing the lot of the angels. Angels are also seen on earth fighting with the Sons of Light. The Gospel records abound in references to angels as instruments of revelation. In Matthew 18:10 Jesus spoke of his "little ones" as having "angels (who) do always behold the face of (His) Father in heaven."

The tendency to exalt angels to a semi-divine position was resisted both by the synagogue and the early church. Paul warned the Colossians against angel-worship (Colossians 2:18). Angelolatry is repudiated in the Book of the Revelation (22: 8 f.). Angels are "ministering spirits" (Hebrews 1:14) and must not usurp the prerogatives of deity.

The orthodox church, however, early adopted the custom of paying reverence to the army of good angels. The custom is mentioned by Justin Martyr in the second century. It became prominent in the life of the medieval church.

The use of magical incantations to procure desired ends is almost universal among primitive peoples. When religion becomes more sophisticated, magic frequently continues at the popular level, even though it is repudiated officially. Like other social customs, magic may cross cultural lines. In fact an incantation in a strange, foreign tongue is frequently more impressive than one in a known language.

The Jews, themselves, after the Persian period developed an extensive magical literature. Never official, this literature seems to have persisted as a kind of "bootleg religion" and left its influence in the early church.

In 1913, the University of Pennsylvania Press published a selection of these texts under the title, *Aramaic Incantation Texts from Nippur,* edited by James A. Montgomery. Others have subsequently been edited, notably by Cyrus H. Gordon, one of Montgomery's disciples.

Indicative of the cosmopolitan nature of this form of magic is the following taken from an Aramaic bowl:

> Let there be health from the heavens, and sealing and guarding unto the dwelling, threshold, residence and house and threshold of this Farukdad son of Zbinta and Qamoy, daughter of Zarq may be preserved: they, their sons, daughters, oxen, asses, slaves, handmaids, all cattle great and small, that there are in this dwelling and threshold or may come to be therein, — that there

may be annulled from this dwelling and threshold of this Farukdad son of Zbinta and Qamoy daughter of Zarq, Aramaean spells, Jewish spells, Arabic spells, Persian spells, Mandaean spells, Greek spells, spells of the Romans, spells that are worked in the seventy languages either by women or men."

Most interesting is the way in which the Babylonian goddess of the netherworld, Eresh-ki-gal, entered magical literature as Erechigag or Ereshchigag. These appear in Gnostic literature from Egypt during the third millennium of the Christian era. The Egyptian god Chnoum, another form of the jackal god Anubis, also appears. In the Gnostic *Pistis Sophia* we meet the combination Zorokothora Melgisedec – Biblical Melchizedek identified with Persian Zoroaster.

This is obviously the popular rather than the normative Judaism, expressing a type of syncretism which accepts "magic" from every imaginable source. Some texts use the names of God in the exorcism of demons. Montgomery's Text #7 exorcises demons "in the name of the Great God, and with the seal of Shadda El and by the splendor of Sabaoth, and by the great glory of the Holy One." The archons who rule the universe according to later Gnosticism often bear Old Testament divine names – Iao, Sabaoth, Adonai, Elohim, El Shaddai. From serving as synonyms for the name of the God of Israel they became proper names for inferior beings. One wonders if the users of the Aramaic bowls regarded the divine names as representing different spiritual entities.

It is interesting to note that the Hebrew name *Yahweh sabaoth*, "Lord of sabaoth," appears in some portions of the Septuagint, notably in Isaiah, as *kurios sabaoth*,which appears to have been interpreted by the ignorant as the name of a divine personage, Lord Sabaoth. F. C. Burkett in his Morse Lectures (1931) argues that this could not have been a Jewish concept because the Jews knew better! The evidence of the incantation bowls argues to the contrary, however.

In some Gnostic systems the name Ialdabaoth appears. While it would be tempting to see in this a corruption of *Yahweh sabaoth*, it more probably comes from a formation such as *Yeled-ab-sabaoth*, perhaps "the child, father of Sabaoth."

Some Aramaic bowls represent great personages of the past as possessing power. Text four states: "I have charmed you with the charm with which Enoch was charmed by his wicked brothers." The name of a great rabbi, Joshua bar Perahia, is frequently invoked as having special power over demons.

The names of angels are likewise potent. Text seven invokes "Gabriel, Michael, and Raphael, and . . . the name of the angel 'Asiel and Ermes' [i.e. Hermes] the Great Lord."

In one of the texts an invocation is given in the form of a rhyming nonsense couplet, a kind of "hocus pocus" or "abracadabra." The so-called nonsense words used in magic probably had a meaning at one time, but the original form and meaning had long been forgotten when the words were used in our texts.

That the atypical, non-normative side of Judaism as represented in the Incantation Texts had some influence upon Gnosticism seems clear. Irenaeus in his work, *Against Heresies,* makes the observation, "Others invoke certain Hebrew names in order to impress the initiates even more, thus, '*Basema chamosse baaiabora, mistadia ruada kousta babophor calachthei.*' "

Although clearly Hebrew in origin, these words have lost all sense of meaning to the Gnostics who used them as a magical formula in connection with their *gnosis.* It may seem a far cry from magical incantations to the Gnosticism which threatened to supplant orthodox Christianity, but there are evident relationships, nevertheless.

III. Observations and Conclusions

Judaism as we know it traces its origin to the Pharisees. The Pharisees were the most influential party in Palestinian Judaism before the destruction of the Temple, A.D. 70. They survived after the Romans had destroyed Jerusalem and, from their Talmudic schools, developed that expression of Judaism which has kept that people together during nineteen centuries. This Pharisaic Judaism is considered normative Judaism. It stressed the study of Torah, the Law, and developed into a system of complicated legalism.

This normative Judaism had little influence beyond its own membership. Destitute of political freedom and always a religious minority, normative Judaism expended its energies in developing and preserving its own traditions, and seeking to keep its members faithful to them. As in the case of the early church, persecutions did not annihilate the Jewish hope, but refined it and made it burn more brightly.

Historically, however, this normative, Pharisaic Judaism was not the only type, either before or after A.D. 70. The influences on the outside world seem to have come largely from this non-normative variety, and for good reason.

The Jews of the dispersion were looked upon with a degree of suspicion by the Jews of the homeland. The fact that they lived in Gentile lands and spoke, for the most part, Greek, made them appear a little less Jewish than their compatriots who chose to live in Palestine. That they frequently were influenced by their Gentile environment needs no proof. The other side of the picture is equally true, however. The Gentile environment was confronted with Judaism. After the third century B.C. the Jewish Scriptures were available in a Greek translation. Consciously or unconsciously, the Jews of the dispersion were missionaries.

It was in the non-normative Jewish circles that the books which we term Apocrypha and Pseudepigrapha became popular. Banned by orthodoxy, they were preserved, first in non-normative Jewish circles, then in the Christian church. Similarly, the Qumran literature, while geographically related to Palestinian Judaism, represented a secession movement, had its own sectarian literature, and renounced as evil the Jewish leaders in Jerusalem. Although highly esteemed by Josephus and the other writers the Essenes are never mentioned in the Jewish Talmud. They were looked upon as an extremist sect. Other non-normative sects and groups had similar histories.

Yet it appears that these non-normative Jews exerted a tremendous influence upon their environment – an influence which is only now being appreciated. As late as the time of Mohammed, non-normative Judaism seems to have been exerting its influence. The knowledge which Mohammed shows of both Judaism and Christianity appears to have come from sources removed from the centers of both Jewish and Christian orthodoxy.

Within the framework of Christianity, the Ebionite movement constitutes a challenging historical problem. Although we do not take seriously the suggestion of Teicher that the Qumran Scrolls are of Ebionite origin, there may be historical connections between the Qumran Essenes and the Jewish-Christian Ebionite sect. The most that could be suggested is that, following the destruction of Jerusalem a part of the Essene community accepted an Ebionite type of Christianity. Even this is conjecture.

Coming closer to Gnosticism, the attitude of Marcion to the Old Testament exhibits a thorough-going anti-Jewish bias. This bias, however, seems to be directed against that type of legalistic Judaism which we have termed Pharisaical, or normative. This does not preclude influences from non-normative Jewish sources on both Marcion and Gnosticism in general.

What became of the non-normative Jewish groups? The answer is manifold. Some certainly joined the main stream of Jewish life. Others, and evidently a sizable number, became Christians, and their traditions merged with those of the church. Others evidently became assimilated into the varied religious and cultural patterns of the Greco-Roman world. Sectarianism did not completely die out of Judaism. The medieval Karaites, stressing loyalty to Scripture and, denying the authority of the rabbis, represent something of a revival of the kind of life emphasized in the Qumran documents.

What does this mean in relation to the Gnostic sects? The non-normative Judaism, as represented by the Qumran community, represented one of those tendencies which came to fruition in Gnosticism. The Qumran scrolls contain no hint of that *gnosis* which liberates a soul from its imprisonment in the world of matter. They do, however, present a well-defined ethical dualism and a vocabulary which indicates trends within Judaism that were moving in the direction of something similar to Gnosticism.

This fact will have an important bearing on New Testament studies, as scholars realize the extent to which Hellenistic thought patterns had been adopted by Jews who considered themselves ultra-orthodox in the two centuries before Christ. Ideas which were deemed late importations in the Christian church because they savoured of Gnosticism must now be studied in the light of their Jewish background.

If our reconstructions are correct, we picture Hellenistic Judaism, including the Qumran community, as the subject of influences from all directions. Although there is a natural resistance to outside influences, some of them are inevitably accepted. Thus a sect like the Essenes, ultra-orthodox in its own eyes, is actually expressing its historic faith in language and thought patterns current during the first two pre-Christian centuries.

These very Essenes, and similar groups, in turn helped to provide a background on which the thought patterns of succeeding centuries were built. From this milieu arose first an incipient form of Gnosticism which appears in the late apostolic age, and finally the full-orbed Gnosticism which was challenged and ultimately overcome by orthodox Christianity.

APPENDIX

CHRONOLOGY

Event		B.C.
Fall of Jerusalem to Nebuchadnezzar		587
Edict of Cyrus permitting return		538
Second (Restoration) Temple Completed		515
Conquest of Alexander the Great		334-323
Syrian Conquest of Palestine		200
High Priest Onias III deposed by Antiochus Epiphanes in favor of Jason		175
Antiochus Epiphanes forces Hellenistic Culture on the Jews The Temple Defiled		168
Mattathias kills an apostate Jew and an officer of Antiochus. Maccabean revolt begins Hasidim co-operate		167
Judas Maccabeus wages guerilla warfare		166-165
The Temple Purified Hasidim satisfied with religious liberty	(Dec. 25)	165
Death of Antiochus Epiphanes		163
Jonathan succeeds Judas, his brother		160-142
Simon, last brother, secures political indepedence for the Jews. Simon's descendants become ruling high priests, establishing the Hasmonean dynasty		142-134
Simon and two sons murdered by Ptolemy, his son-in-law		134
John Hyrcanus, Simon's 3rd son Rift with the Pharisees Building of Qumran buildings		134-104
Aristobulus I, son of Hyrcanus Had mother and brother killed		104-103

Kept three brothers in prison Took title "King"	
Alexander Jannaeus Brother of Aristobulus Freed from prison by Aristobulus' widow Alexandra who then married Jannaeus Bitter enemy of Pharisees Civil war, 94-89 B.C.	103-76
Alexandra Widow of Aristobulus and Jannaeus Son Hyrcanus II named High Priest Sympathetic to Pharisees Reforms in education	76-67
Aristobulus II Son of Alexandra Rivalry with Hyrcanus II	66-63
Romans, under Pompey, intervene End of independent Jewish state	63
Hyrcanus II High Priest under Romans Aristobulus II taken to Rome	63-40
Antigonus II Last son of Aristobulus II Placed on throne by Parthians – enemies of Rome Executed by order of Mark Anthony	40-37
Herod the Great Earthquake 31 B.C. Qumran abandoned	37-4
Herod Archelaus Restoration of Community at Qumran	4 B.C.-A.D. 6
Roman Procurators Pontius Pilate (A.D. 26-36)	A.D. 6-41
Herod Agrippa I Made King by Caligula Ruled part of Palestine from A.D. 37	41-44
Roman Procurators Return Herod Agrippa II, king over sections of Galilee and Peraca (A.D. 59-93)	44-66
Jewish Revolt against Rome Destruction of Qumran by Vespasian, A.D. 68 Titus destroys Jerusalem, A.D. 70	66-70

Qumran occupied as Roman Military Outpost	c. 68-c. 100

Second Jewish (Bar Kochba) Revolt
  Qumran occupied by Jewish forces
  Roman authority re-established
  Jerusalem rebuilt as a Roman colony, Aelia Capitolina, but closed to the Jews.
	132-135

INDEX OF NAMES AND SUBJECTS